DEC

D0429522

PRAISE FOR *WOKE CHURCH*

Eric Mason gives insight on societal, racial, and theological matters with proficiency. This book is a rare gem; few leaders are as competent and scholarly in how to address the divides and conflicts in society that greatly affect the church. This is a book I'll share for generations.

LECRAE
Grammy awarding winning artist @lecrae

After thirty-five years of local church ministry, I cannot think of a better word to describe the need of today than *woke*. What if the church really woke up to its power in Christ, and its position in the world? Let the prophetic ministry of Dr. Eric Mason rally your heart to God's priority on earth, a church that is wide awake to the needs all around them and what Jesus Christ still wants to accomplish.

JAMES MACDONALD
Founding and Senior Pastor of Harvest Bible Chapel

So incredibly thankful for Eric. *Woke Church* is a timely and thought-provoking work to help us in these important times. He does an amazing job of giving us fresh perspective on the intersection of justice, race, and the gospel. Our culture is crying for a gospel-centered conversation on matters of race and justice. *Woke Church* is an instant classic that will help us both individually and collectively grasp the great opportunity before us to live out the gospel in these important times.

BRYAN CARTER
Senior Pastor of Concord Church and codeveloper of "33—The Series"

Woke Church is a clarion call of love—the love that is at the heart of the gospel of Jesus Christ. It is a word of knowledge long overdue for the evangelical context in the secular age. Mason talks with a tone that should mitigate the perceived fatigue factor that often leads to backlash, hostility, and/or dismissal on discussions of the gospel's implications for social and racial justice. Readers—those already woke and still asleep alike—who care for the souls of people perishing all around them should be moved to act with a sense of urgency for God-centered righteousness in society after embracing the Christ-consciousness of this great work.

ERIC C. REDMOND
Associate Professor of Bible, Moody Bible Institute

Woke Church is a seriously important book dealing with a core applicational issue in the church and in our society today. It is seriously biblical, showing the connections between reconciliation, justice, love, and the gospel. What God has joined together should not be seated and the church as a multiethnic, multinational body needs to better reflect what God designed it to be. This book helps us think through how to get there.

DARRELL BOCK
Executive Director of Cultural Engagement and Senior Research Professor of New Testament Studies at Dallas Theological Seminary

Growing up in an all-white context in the Midwest, but now a part of a multicultural church, I've had to do much work to gain clarity on justice and race issues. I am thankful for Dr. Mason's work showing practical ways we can cultivate meaningful relationships that would cause the church to have an immense impact on this broken world, bringing true justice and true peace.

RACHAEL TURNER
Church planting wife, local church member, Living Stones, Reno, NV

Dr. Eric Mason has done it. In a day and age when the church is looking to halt its increasing marginalization within mainstream society, seeking answers (like the rest of America) to our nation's still troublesome problem of racial division and injustice, and desperately hoping to gain disciples among the young, Dr. Mason provides the answer: we need to be "woke." Not just the Blacks, not just the millennials, not just the left-leaning, but all of us. The entire Bible-believing body of Christ needs to wake up to the fullness of the gospel message—that Christ died to reconcile man to God and man to man, or in other words, that Jesus has called us to strive for both personal morality and societal justice. If the church remains stubborn and "asleep," it could soon find itself completely locked out of the public discourse. If it heeds the words of Dr. Mason, it could be empowered to spark revival.

CHRIS BROUSSARD
FOX Sports Television Analyst and Commentator
Founder and President of The K.I.N.G. Movement

The Lord neither slumbers nor sleeps. But not so His church. We have constant need of being told to "wake up, you sleeper" and to "keep watch." We are like those first disciples in Gethsemane, spirit willing, flesh weak, falling over on our post. Sadly this has been true of the church when it comes to racism and injustice. We need an urgent call, a quickened conscience, an enlivened heart, a clear vision, and working hands to prophetically address with gospel power the ails of the church and the society. Dr. Eric Mason has thought as much about this as anyone in our day and we have much to glean from this clarion call to wake up and rep Christ!

THABITI ANYABWILE
Pastor of Anacostia River Church in Washington, D.C.
Council member of The Gospel Coalition

While I barely missed the sixties, perusing the current milieu makes me feel as if we are back in those turbulent times. Another black body slain in the streets. Cops called on people of color for walking in their own neighborhoods. Divisive rhetoric from 1600 Pennsylvania Avenue. Silent evangelicals muted by their own incomplete theology. It's time for the church to awake! My friend Dr. Eric Mason not only diagnoses the problem but provides tangible solutions for the people of God to walk in Christ-exalting unity. I believe when the dust is settled, *Woke Church* will be regarded as a seminal tome in what it means to be the church.

BRYAN LORITTS
Author, *Insider/Outsider*

I'm excited about *Woke Church*. My son in the ministry has written a classic theological and practical work that will aid the church in a paradigm shift as it pertains to the brokenness that is in our country today. Eric is a prophetic biblical voice the entire church needs to hear. Read this work and be inspired to renew your commitment to seeing Jesus work in our sphere to challenge and even change racial injustice in America.

TONY EVANS
Senior Pastor, Oak Cliff Bible Fellowship
President, The Urban Alternative

Any objective reading of the New Testament should bring the reader to the conclusion that God has a great love for the world. This love is demonstrated through the giving of his son who was the prophetic fulfillment of Isaiah 42—a servant of God who would bring justice to the world. A biblically balanced soteriology and ecclesiology always has sociological implications. A lack of balance between righteousness and justice is not only unbiblical, it's dangerous. It abdicates our responsibility to be salt in the earth and the light of the world. It's an expression of Christianity that allowed and in some cases endorsed the atrocities of slavery and the Jim Crow South. In this incredible work, Dr. Eric Mason calls the church out of her sleep and slumber and awakens her to her biblical responsibility to not only address the sins in our hearts but also in our systems. He passionately and masterfully reminds us of what the Lord requires; to act justly, love mercy, and walk humbly before our God. This book is not only a gift to the church, it is a gift to the world.

DHARIUS DANIELS
Lead Pastor, Change Church
Author, *RePresent Jesus*

Woke Church is a desperately needed, biblically brilliant, pivotal work by my pastor, Dr. Mason. Confronting the often ignored challenge of applying the gospel of Jesus Christ to modern conceptions of race, the pages of *Woke Church* bleed with a pastoral passion to transform the church's view on race. Read this book and let it read you. Learn from one of the most prophetic voices of our time. With prophetic, pastoral, and biblical insights, *Woke Church* will confront and emotionally engage every reader. This powerful message of hope and healing is a must read that will be treasured for generations.

DOUG LOGAN JR.
Codirector of Church in Hard Places and Director of Diversity for the Acts29 Network; author of *On The Block: Developing a Biblical Picture for Missional Engagement*

Dr. Eric Mason has done something remarkable in writing *Woke Church*. From the very first page to the last, you will experience the wisdom and expertise of a theologian, pastor, and cultural architect who practices what he preaches. Buy this book. You will not regret it. It's time for the church in America to wake up. Dr. Mason is sounding the alarm clock.

DERWIN L. GRAY
Lead Elder-Pastor, Transformation Church
Author of *The High Definition Leader: Building Multiethnic Churches in a Multiethnic World*

This book is needed and Dr. Eric Mason is the one to write it. Eric is both a theologically astute pastor and a practitioner of the content. In our current cultural climate, this book will help to serve church leaders as they think through the implications of the gospel in church and society. Thoroughly biblical, rooted in history, powerful.

HARVEY TURNER
Founder of the Living Stones Family of Churches
Acts 29 US West Leadership Team

In 1933, Dr. Carter G. Woodson, the father of Black History, wrote a transformative book that questioned the effectiveness of the educational system in America for black people, called *The Mis-Education of the Negro*. Unfortunately his analysis and critique is still relevant today. In the same brilliance as Dr. Woodson, Dr. Eric Mason has written a book that I believe will be transformative for many years to come. *Woke Church* is written in a manner that provides an accurate historical and philosophical critique, while at the same time it constructs a biblical perspective that is needed. It is a must read in order to correct the dangerous mis-education of the church.

JAMES WHITE
Executive Vice President, YMCA of the Triangle

By highlighting the comprehensive power of the gospel to not only change individual lives but to transform communities, Dr. Mason compels the American church to take a hard look at its complicity in the development of racial inequality and issues a clarion call for the church to confront injustice in all of its forms. However, *Woke Church* does more than just reveal the church's shortcomings, but provides practical and Scripture-based solutions. It's a must read!

TIFFANY M. GILL
Scholar, writer, and professor of African American History

Many still see the gospel and justice as being mutually exclusive. Dr. Mason challenges this notion. He helps us to recognize that the gospel calls us to stand for justice. Not only does Dr. Mason push us toward the presence of God in lament, he also calls us to step into the presence and experiences of those impacted by racism.

JUMAINE JONES
Lead Pastor of The Bridge, Silver Spring, MD
Author of *Lost in Love: Navigating the Five Relationship Terrains*

ERIC MASON

WOKE CHURCH

AN URGENT CALL FOR CHRISTIANS IN AMERICA TO CONFRONT RACISM AND INJUSTICE

MOODY PUBLISHERS

CHICAGO

All Scripture quotations, unless otherwise indicated, are taken from the *Christian Standard Bible*® (CSB), copyright © 1999, 1962, 2000, 2002, 2003, 2009 by Holman Bible Publishers. Used by permission.

Scripture quotations marked ESV are from The ESV® Bible (The Holy Bible, English Standard Version®), copyright © 2001 by Crossway, a publishing ministry of Good News Publishers. Used by permission. All rights reserved.

Scripture quotations marked NASB are taken from the New American Standard Bible® (NASB), Copyright © 1960, 1962, 1963, 1968, 1971, 1972, 1973, 1975, 1977, 1995 by The Lockman Foundation. Used by permission. www.Lockman.org.

Scripture quotations marked NIV are taken from the Holy Bible, New International Version®, NIV®. Copyright © 1973, 1978, 1984, 2011 by Biblica, Inc.™ Used by permission of Zondervan. All rights reserved worldwide. www.zondervan.com The "NIV" and "New International Version" are trademarks registered in the United States Patent and Trademark Office by Biblica, Inc.™015

Scripture quotations marked NKJV are taken from the New King James Version. Copyright © 1982 by Thomas Nelson. Used by permission. All rights reserved.

Scripture quotations marked KJV are taken from the King James Version.

Emphasis to Scripture has been added.

Published in association with the literary agency of Wolgemuth & Associates.

Edited by: Karen Waddles
Interior design: Erik M. Peterson
Cover design: Joshua Dingle - LoveArts Inc.
Author photo: Rightnow Media
Illustration of scales courtesy of Icons8 (icons8.com)Illustration of lion by Josh Dingle

Library of Congress Cataloging-in-Publication Data

Names: Mason, Eric (Eric M.), author.
Title: Woke church : an urgent call for Christians in America to confront racism and injustice / Eric Mason.
Description: Chicago : Moody Publishers, 2018. | Includes bibliographical references.
Identifiers: LCCN 2018031606 (print) | LCCN 2018035650 (ebook) | ISBN 9780802496577 (ebook) | ISBN 9780802416988
Subjects: LCSH: United States--Church history--21st century. | United States--Race relations. | Race relations--Religious aspects--Christianity. | Racism--United States. | Racism--Religious aspects--Christianity. | Christianity and justice--United States.
Classification: LCC BR526 (ebook) | LCC BR526 .M365 2018 (print) | DDC 277.3/083089--dc23
LC record available at https://lccn.loc.gov/2018031606

We hope you enjoy this book from Moody Publishers. Our goal is to provide high-quality, thought-provoking books and products that connect truth to your real needs and challenges. For more information on other books and products written and produced from a biblical perspective, go to www.moodypublishers.com or write to:

Moody Publishers
820 North LaSalle Boulevard
Chicago, IL 60610

1 3 5 7 9 10 8 6 4 2

Printed in the United States of America

To the late Jimmie Lee Mason, my earthly father. From being born and raised in the Jim Crow south to fighting in WWII and the Korean War and winning two purple hearts and returning to a country that didn't acknowledge your full humanity, I salute you. You endured so much and still managed to find ways to warn us to speak redemptively. It blows my mind. I dedicate this book to your memory and legacy. 1923–2017

CONTENTS

FOREWORD

John M. Perkins

I can still vividly remember what life was like growing up as a black boy in southern Mississippi in the 1930s and '40s. In our little town, when we saw a white man and woman coming down the sidewalk, we stepped to the side and let them get by. Everything was separate. There were separate theaters, separate waiting rooms, separate water fountains. There were even separate restrooms. And while there were restrooms for white men and white women, there was just one for blacks—and it was never cleaned.

My mother died when I was seven months old and the police killed my brother when I was a boy. But it wasn't until I was badly beaten in a Brandon jail that I saw the absolute necessity for reconciliation. It was there that I saw the depths of racism. I wanted nothing to do with white people after that. But while I recovered in the hospital, white doctors and nurses cared for me, washing my wounds and loving me. We were healing each other. That's when I prayed, "Lord, I want to preach a gospel that can reconcile, that brings blacks and whites together in one body."

But before I started striving for reconciliation, I had to face the horrors of racism. Today I worry that we've forgotten our past and remain in denial about many of the challenges we face in the present. There's a tendency to want to gloss over injustices for the sake of unity. However, any authentic attempt to pursue unity and reconciliation must start with truth. The journey toward healing begins with an awakening.

That's why I'm grateful for *Woke Church*. In this important book, Eric Mason sounds a clarion call for the church. No longer can we remain asleep to the injustice in our past and present. No longer can we afford to see justice issues as separate from the gospel. No longer can we wait for someone else to do the hard work of reconciliation. This may be an uncomfortable book for some people to read. Eric explores the roots of racial injustice in our history and argues that the forces that drive us apart are still alive and well in our midst. But he has a pastor's heart and an abiding love for Christ's church. He makes his case with faith and hope, with an eye toward the glorious future described in the book of Revelation, where people from every tribe and tongue will gather around the throne of Jesus and worship Him together.

In his letter to the Ephesians, the apostle Paul wrote:

> "Awake, O sleeper,
>   and arise from the dead,
> and Christ will shine on you." (5:14 ESV)

Paul was challenging the church to throw off their old ways and walk in the light. We still need this call. I'm grateful that my brother Eric is sounding it afresh in our day and I pray that the church will listen.

JOHN M. PERKINS
Founder of the John and Vera Mae Perkins Foundation, co-founder of the Christian Community Development Association, and author of *One Blood: Parting Words to the Church on Race*

FOREWORD

LIGON DUNCAN

I am about the least "woke" person you could meet. I have spent much of my life in a haze of relative cluelessness about and culpable indifference to many of the concerns that are addressed in this book. For instance, having grown up in South Carolina during the Civil Rights era, when I came to Jackson, Mississippi, at the age of twenty-nine, to teach systematic theology at Reformed Theological Seminary in the summer of 1990, the very first course I was asked to teach was "Pastoral and Social Ethics." Now which, you may ask, social issues did I choose to address in the course? Abortion? Check. Homosexuality? Check. Marriage, divorce and remarriage? Check. Medical ethics (infertility, end of life issues, etc.)? Check. Just war? Check. Death penalty? Check.

But what about racism? Um, no. It did not even occur to me that this was a pastoral issue that I needed to prepare future ministers to address biblically in the church, much less in the communities where they would serve. How in the world could I have missed that? How could I have been so utterly blind to my context? How did a sin that had pervaded my whole world growing up not even register to me as something to help preachers address, especially considering that many of them were going to minister in places where overt racism in the church [e.g., majority white churches denying membership to black Christians] was still an ongoing reality? See what I mean? Not woke.

So, why did Dr. Eric Mason invite me to write the foreword to this book (especially alongside a spiritual giant like Dr. John Perkins)? And why did I accept? Did Dr. Mason have a momentary lapse of good judgment? Well, possibly so, but let me defend him for a moment. At Together for the Gospel in Louisville in 2018, I preached a message called "The Whole in Our Holiness." Dr. Mason heard that message, and asked me to join Dr. Perkins in writing the foreword to this book. What did I say in that sermon? Among other things, I asserted that in my own theological tradition (the mainstream American conservative Protestant tradition—Presbyterians, Congregationalists, Baptists, Episcopalians, etc.), the application of what Jesus called the second greatest commandment, to love our neighbor, has been both deliberately and unwittingly truncated in one particular area. Specifically, during the eras of slavery, segregation, and civil rights, some of our best theological minds figured out how "love your neighbor" did NOT apply to the racism and injustice (and, by the way, I mean injustice the way the Bible defines injustice) that black people were experiencing, oftentimes at the hands of professed Christians, in both church and community. I then suggested that racial tensions in our churches and our nation would be in a significantly better state if the Reformed community in America in the nineteenth and twentieth centuries had simply rightly applied the second great commandment. But tragically, the Reformed community—my community, my people—devised ways to limit its application.

Now, there's more to it than that, but I'm writing a foreword, not a book. Suffice it to say, I think Dr. Mason realized that that sermon was in part the fruit of the Lord patiently working on me for the last thirty years or so, to open my eyes from my own blindness, and he knew I would benefit from his own experience with and exposition of these matters in this book, and could thoroughly commend it to others.

But why did I accept his gracious invitation to join Dr. Perkins in writing the foreword? Well, for many reasons, chief among them my respect for Dr. Mason as a faithful gospel preacher who loves and believes the inspired, inerrant, infallible, authoritative Word of God, and who is a transcendent voice in this larger discussion. There are many people out there today speaking to the issues addressed in this book, but they are doing so in unbiblical, uninformed, and unwise ways. Many, even well-meaning Christians, are speaking to these issues in ways that unnecessarily divide and confuse. Dr. Mason's voice is one trying to bring us together.

My colleague at Reformed Theological Seminary, Karen Ellis, always says to me: "we need transcendent voices" addressing this, voices that rise above the fray, above petty bickering, voices that refuse partisan mantras that are simple and appealing but wrong and unhelpful, voices rooted in the Word of God that understand the times, that faithfully speak truth into our current context, help us understand ourselves, our neighbors, our challenges, and the way forward. Dr. Mason is such a voice. I look forward to sitting at his feet to listen and learn.

LIGON DUNCAN
Chancellor/CEO Reformed Theological Seminary; John E. Richards Professor of Systematic and Historical Theology

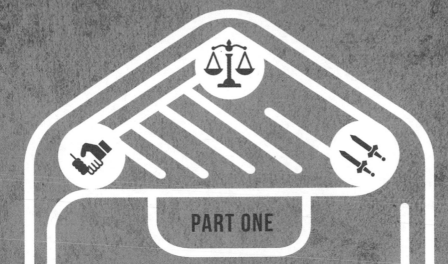

PART ONE

BE AWARE

THE CHURCH SHOULD ALREADY BE WOKE

The Kilauea Volcano in Hawaii erupted on May 17, 2018 at 4:17 a.m. spewing lava more than a thousand feet in the air. Homes and other structures in the wake of the lava flow and the eruption's related ongoing events were destroyed. But geologists say that the volcano has been erupting almost continuously since 1983.[1] One eruption is followed by a period of calm . . . maybe another year or so of quiet that allows people to relax and forget . . . and then another eruption. Because volcanoes are formed when a tectonic plate shifts over a hot spot in the layers of earth beneath the surface, we never know exactly when or where they will erupt.

The issues of racism and injustice are like that Kilauea Volcano in a lot of ways. They form a hotbed of lava that lives just beneath the surface, and at any moment, they can explode violently—as happened in Charleston, South Carolina when Dylan Roof went into a black church and gunned down ten worshippers.

Or these issues can fuel the subtle micro-aggressions that minorities experience on a daily basis, like being ignored when they go into shops for service, or being followed because people assume they are stealing.

But the evangelical church seems to be asleep to the hotbed of tensions that threatens to overflow into communities across America. Scripture makes it clear that we are supposed to be totally awake to what is happening in our world and steadfast in our commitment to fulfill the great commandments. Jesus fulfilled the law by calling for a love of God and neighbor. Although this is supposed to be a lifestyle that characterizes all Christians, we have to be called to this over and over again as a prophetic community. In Ephesians 5:13–14, Paul says,

> Everything *exposed* by the light is made visible, for what makes everything visible is light. Therefore, it is said: *Get up, sleeper,* and *rise up from the dead,* and Christ will shine on you.

When Paul talks about everything being "exposed by the light," this doesn't merely mean to see something that was hidden. It is deeper than that. The word for exposed means "rebuke, expose; refute, show one's fault, implying that there is a convincing of that fault."[2]

What Paul is saying is that the gospel strengthens us through the Spirit to see things in our society that others do not. We are called, as the people of God, to wake up. To see what others don't and call it out. The church in America is not awake to the reality of what is happening in communities across this nation, and we are missing out on our calling to shine the light into these places of darkness for Christ's glory.

CNN released an exclusive report in October 2017 titled,

"People for Sale: Where Lives Are Auctioned for $400."[3] A team of their reporters traveled to Libya and witnessed smugglers auctioning off twelve migrant men as slaves, some for no more than $400. This modern-day slavery sprang up in recent years when the Libyan coast guard started cracking down on refugees fleeing the country for Europe. Smugglers suddenly had a backlog of refugees on their hands and began selling them as slaves. The reporters learned of at least nine other locations in the country where these auctions were taking place.

As our family sat around the family table for dinner, we started talking about what was happening in Libya. We often discuss current events around the dinner table, assessing them through a biblical worldview. My sons came and stood up behind me as I took out my phone. We don't usually allow phones at the dinner table, but I made an exception this time. I began showing them a video, not of atrocities, but of the reporting on the story so they could see and understand what was happening.

My eight-year-old son, Nehemiah, started crying. He said, "Who are these people?"

I said, "Son, these are our people."

He said, "These are *our* people? Is this *today*?" He could not wrap his eight-year-old mind around it. He began to weep because he could not reconcile the idea of slavery in today's age.

My son couldn't believe that people of any kind would be enslaved, particularly people that looked like him. Nehemiah had never been to Libya. He had never met any of the people featured in the video that we watched, but they looked like him, and he immediately understood his connection to them. They were *his* people. And their pain, their trauma, became his pain and trauma. When I think about his emotional response, I see what should happen within the family of God whenever injustice rears its ugly head.

I'm so grateful that God saved us to be in relationship with Him. But He also bought us to be in relationship with one another. God's intent is for us to hurt with one another, to care about the suffering of one another. When I think of Nehemiah's tears, I have to wonder when such lament will come from the church body of our white brothers and sisters . . . where is the collective voice, the emotive, empathetic, impassioned cry in response to their black brothers and sisters who are suffering and experiencing trauma?

It's one thing if a stranger gets shot on the street. We feel for them; we may even pray for them. But when somebody you have a relationship with gets shot, there's a different response because of their nearness, because of connection, because of love. Our division in the church in America is rooted in disconnection from one another. And that, my Christian brothers and sisters, should not be.

When Christ returns, all of our bylaws and documents for our organizations will dissolve. We will be consumed with knowing Him and knowing one another. My urgent plea to the church is that we begin to let that future truth impact our present reality.

On one of my favorite shows, there was an interview that Oprah did with rapper and businessman Jay-Z. She asked Jay-Z for his perspective on race, and as he began to talk I found myself feeling convicted. He said that hip-hop, through its music and its culture, has had more impact on race relations than any figure or any entity other than Martin Luther King Jr. and the Civil Rights movement. He talked about how whites and blacks can come together in the clubs—even though they might not get together outside the club. They gather around this musical and cultural form and find solace in being able to talk about things they wouldn't normally talk about. Hip-hop helped them to start talking with one another and even to begin building relationships.

Why was I convicted by that? Because a musical, cultural form that's only about forty years old should not have more impact than the church, which has existed for thousands of years. We should be the main communicator about challenges that happen in our country on race and justice. We should be the first place that people look to for answers. We should be the ones presenting a clear, viable model of the hope that lies within us.

We all have that hope, the hope that Jesus provides. Whether we are black, white, Haitian, Asian, African, or European Christians, we should have a unified voice. We're all people of the same Bible, even though we're in different locations and have different ethnicities. But we have the same blood, the same Holy Ghost, the same Word! We should already be *woke* to what is happening in our world. And we should be shouting His message about it from the mountaintops.

WHAT DO YOU MEAN BY WOKE?

My desire in this book is to encourage the church to utilize the mind of Christ and to be fully awake to the issues of race and injustice in this country. Pan-Africanists and Black Nationalists use the term "woke" to refer to no longer being naïve nor in mental slavery. We have borrowed the term and redeemed it to be used in the context of being awakened from deadened, sinful thinking. In fact, every believer has been awakened from sin's effects and Satan's deception (Eph. 5:14). Thus, the believer is able to be aware of sin and challenge it wherever it is.

Woke is a word commonly used by those in the black community as a term for being socially aware of issues that have systemic impact. This social awareness doesn't come from just watching the news or reading history through a traditional lens. Being woke has to do with seeing all of the issues and being able to connect cultural, socio-economic, philosophical, historical, and ethical dots. A similar term is *conscious*.

Here's how one commentator describes being woke:

> To me staying woke means making sure that you're
> tuned into your community. That you are doing every-
> thing that you can to not only educate yourself but to
> bring someone else along. To ensure that we all have the
> same information. It's not enough to be woke on your
> own; you need to help someone else along to also get
> woke. Woke is about a state of mind.[4]

Both *conscious* and *woke* find their beginnings in the writings of William Edward Burghardt ("W. E. B.") Du Bois, the great
twentieth-century father of sociology. He spoke of a *double consciousness*. Du Bois speaks of being woke in terms of the double
consciousness of black people in his landmark work, *The Souls of
Black Folk:*

> the Negro is a sort of seventh son, born with a veil, and
> gifted with second-sight in this American world—a
> world which yields him no true self-consciousness, but
> only lets him see himself through the revelation of the
> other world. It is a peculiar sensation, this double-
> consciousness, this sense of always looking at one's self
> through the eyes of others, of measuring one's soul by
> the tape of a world that looks on in amused contempt
> and pity. One ever feels his two-ness—an American, a
> Negro; two souls, two thoughts, two unreconciled
> strivings; two warring ideals in one dark body, whose
> dogged strength alone keeps it from being torn asunder.
> The history of the American Negro is the history of this
> strife—this longing to attain self-conscious manhood, to
> merge his double self into a better and truer self.[5]

This double consciousness that Du Bois identifies is the struggle of blacks in America. It is a struggle to emerge with a strong sense of self and dignity, while being fully aware of the perception of our people in the eyes of white America. Most African Americans have had at least two life-altering experiences that are burned into their memory—the moment they realized they were black and the moment they realized that was a problem.

Double consciousness is a reality for minorities in this country. But I would like to add a third consciousness to this conversation. This third consciousness is what being truly woke is rooted in. Being truly woke is rooted in Christ Consciousness. This is the anchor. This is the common ground. At our core, without being conscious in Christ, our souls are still in bondage and can only see things from the natural, fleshly appearance. Our Christ Consciousness gives the double consciousness depth and character. Our Christ Consciousness elevates our awareness to our responsibility to care for and love our brothers—even those who don't look like us.

However, if one is regenerated by the gospel, yet unaware of the double consciousness of African Americans and other ethnic minorities in America, one's clarity on justice and race issues will be clouded and even absent. Therefore, to be fully woke, one needs to have all three aspects of consciousness.

Being woke isn't limited to color or ethnicity or culture. It is possible for anyone to be woke. If you have a level of understanding of the double consciousness of blacks and are regenerate, you are woke. However, our dilemma is this: sin and strongholds in our thinking can impair the depths of our wokeness. I celebrate my white siblings who have grappled with and taken hold of this message. You give me hope. I was encouraged by one of these woke brothers awhile back when a young black man was shot and killed by a police officer. My friend Matt Chandler sent an email to me and a few other black pastors saying, "Yo, E, I'm sorry about what happened. I don't know what to say. I'm brokenhearted. Love you guys." He was sensitive to how every time one of these events takes place, it re-traumatizes our communities. That's a woke brother.

I've designed the following chart to help identify how these three aspects of consciousness intersect and impact the psyche of African Americans and specifically African American Christians. It's of critical importance for the broader community to understand the triple consciousness of their black siblings. There are extremes in each area of wokeness, but where all of them intersect—at the cross of Jesus Christ—there is awesome power.

I arrived at this chart after a good number of conversations and research to help define the impact each of these perceptions has on one another and in concert with each other. Having said that, it is not my intent to color anyone with a broad stroke or to suggest that all of these markers are true for every individual in a particular category. My goal is to help the broader community understand the triple consciousness of black Christians. Anything we can do to help ourselves understand and empathize with one another will be beneficial for our witness.

The following chart is not categorically monolithic or static; there are several places of overlap in these categories. My point isn't to over-stereotype, but give the general, overarching themes and different, dominant thought patterns that are pervasive and possible in the black community.

Similarly, my friend, Brian Loritts, tackles this issue in his book *Right Color, Wrong Culture: The Type of Leader Your Organization Needs to Become Multiethnic*. In the book, he makes this statement: "Within every ethnicity there exists at least three cultural expressions."[6] He identifies C1s as people who have fully assimilated into another culture. C3s are culturally inflexible—solidly entrenched in their own culture. And C2s are culturally flexible and adaptable without becoming ethnically ambiguous or hostile.

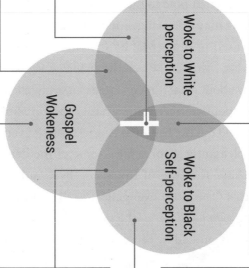

Woke to White perception

Gospel Wokeness

Woke to Black Self-perception

- I believe that the gospel changes our souls and circumstances.
- I believe that many American Christians are culturally captive to their political identities.
- I am unapologetically black and unashamedly Christian.
- I am willing to work on reconciling with whites.
- My spiritual identity is found in Jesus.
- My physical identity and features are created and valued by God.
- I don't have to become another ethnicity to be valued.
- I believe blacks need to create institutions.
- I am not color blind.
- I believe that Christian history needs to be redeemed from white revisionists.
- I fight for unity in the church.

- My sense of self is defined by how the white world perceives me.

- I see myself through the lens of the white Christian world.
- I don't think that systemic racism exists any longer.
- I believe blacks are to blame for our current condition.
- My theology has been developed solely in white spheres.
- I seek white approval for my significance, dignity, and identity.
- I measure other blacks by white cultural standards.

- I seek dignity in the black community.
- I'm more than your categories.
- I have value.
- I don't trust whites.
- I see hypocrisy in American Christianity.

- I believe we should just preach the gospel.
- I don't believe the gospel promotes social engagement.
- I believe the gospel, but don't believe it speaks to racism and injustice.
- I view color blindness as a virtue.

- I view most whites with suspicion.
- I believe that Christianity is the white man's religion.
- I want to be separate from all white institutions.
- I find my significance, dignity, and identity in my African heritage.
- I believe blacks need nationality beyond American citizenship.
- I am likely to be involved in black mystery religions, ideologies or black atheism

- I'm done with Evangelicalism.
- I'm disillusioned with Christianity at times.
- I want to remain Christian, but separate from whites and white Christians.
- I identify more ethically with unbelieving woke blacks than Christians.
- I am partial to black scholarship.
- I believe that Jesus was black.

FULLY EVANGELICAL

I believe that the call of God on the life of every evangelical Christian is to be woke. But today evangelicalism is hard to define. I remember entering Dallas Seminary and hearing that term and needing help. I didn't have a frame of reference for it. You can pose this question to many Christians, and you'll get differing answers. For some Christians, it may be a code word for healthy, trustworthy, biblical Christianity. For other Christians cross ethnically, it is, for the most part, very confusing.

Evangelicalism was defined for me as the covenant community of believers that hold to the historic Christian faith at its core— although we may differ on some nonessentials. Being evangelical has been used in times past by Christians to distinguish who is an orthodox Christian. Over the past few years, there's less and less clarity about what it means to be an evangelical. The term has taken on a political agenda that has become disturbing for many.

I checked out the National Association of Evangelicals (NAE) and was pleasantly surprised by some of the items that were on their website. The core of the evangelical faith is the gospel of Jesus Christ. The word evangelical itself comes from the Greek word *euangelion*, meaning "the good news" or the "gospel." Evangelicals are identified by these four primary characteristics:

- Conversionism: the belief that lives need to be transformed through a "born-again" experience and a life-long process of following Jesus
- Activism: the expression and demonstration of the gospel in missionary and social reform efforts
- Biblicism: a high regard for and obedience to the Bible as the ultimate authority
- Crucicentrism: a stress on the sacrifice of Jesus Christ on the cross as making possible the redemption of humanity.[7]

I fully agree with these statements and believe that the gospel is of first importance, as the apostle Paul strongly asserts:

> Now I want to make clear for you, brothers and sisters, the gospel I preached to you, which you received, on which you have taken your stand and by which you are being saved, if you hold to the message I preached to you—unless you believed in vain. For I passed on to you as most important what I also received: that Christ died for our sins according to the Scriptures.
> (1 Cor. 15:1–3)

I believe that with all of my heart, with all of my mind, and with all of my strength. However, it was the second characteristic of evangelicalism that was especially exciting to me: activism. I longed to hear them flesh out what is meant by "expression and demonstration of the gospel in missionary and social reforms." I wonder how and why this key tenet of evangelicalism has been left undone when the needs are huge and desperate. Many of us are regeneration-focused in a way that ignores the outworking of new life in the world. Historically, when it comes to race and justice, conservative evangelical Christianity didn't have a theology by and large that moved them toward activism.

In the book of Titus, Paul applies regeneration to the area of comprehensive societal engagement. He lets his readers know that they need to be ready for every good work in their city (3:14). "Let our people learn to devote themselves to good works for pressing needs, so that they will not be unfruitful." *Pressing needs*? Pressing needs are those things that are absolutely essential and vitally necessary, indispensable. We can't deny that Paul sees meeting pressing needs as a core Christian commitment; not a peripheral one. We do not substitute proclaiming for action;

and we don't proclaim and neglect action. We proclaim and engage in activism that flows from the gospel.

GOSPEL JUSTICE RESTORATION AND RECIPROCITY CYCLE

To apply this we must be awakened to the reality of implicit and explicit racism and injustice in our society. Until then, our prophetic voice on these matters will be anemic and silent. *Being woke is to be aware. Being woke is to acknowledge the truth. Being woke is to be accountable. Being woke is to be active.* This is the call of God on the church and on every believer. The remainder of this book will be arranged around these four themes. *Be Aware. Be Willing to Acknowledge. Be Accountable. Be Active.*

The following chart pictures what I refer to as the Gospel Justice Restoration and Reciprocity Cycle. This cycle is a recurring process throughout life. Understanding that is helpful for us all. It is no different than how our souls are in a constant cycle of

transformation and spiritual growth. That is: sin, hearing the Word, conviction, confession, repentance, faith, and fruits of transformation. And the cycle starts all over again.

May God's Holy Spirit open our eyes to the places where sin resides, and then provide the healing balm of the Word to stir us and move us together as a Woke Church.

Be Aware. This whole issue of justice has been a contentious one for the church historically. But there is so much that unites us as the family of God. My prayer is that these overarching truths will carry us along on our journey to becoming a Woke Church.

What should connect the church in a vital way to the issue of justice is the imperative of the Gospel. In **Chapter 2: How Big Is the Gospel? (Justice and the Gospel)**, we'll examine what the gospel encompasses. In Matthew 23:23, Jesus rebukes the scribes and Pharisees for their fastidiousness in tithing and their woeful neglect of the more important matters of the law—justice and mercy. He lets them know that in all of their work to understand Yahweh, they have missed justice. We'll talk about the gospel and justice, justice in God's character, justice in the gospel, and justice as the character of the church.

God has called the church to be His representatives in the world . . . but not as a divided body. A Woke Church is One Church. In **Chapter 3: We're Family, We're Holy**, we'll examine what it means for the church to be a family. The apostle Paul wrote the letter to Philemon, a slave owner, to challenge him to forgive and reconcile with his escaped slave, Onesimus, based on their shared connection through Christ. The letter ends up undermining the very foundation of slavery. Where there was only a master–slave relationship before, there is now a family relationship. They are brothers in Christ. They are family, but not just any kind of family. The church is set apart to be holy in this world. We'll talk about that.

Be Willing to Acknowledge. One of the most difficult things for me to deal with is the refusal for many evangelicals to acknowledge the truths about what has happened in our country. Our history has been hard for people of color, and the church must be willing to acknowledge those hard truths if we are to move toward healing. Much of our history is shrouded in darkness because it is hard to talk about and even harder to understand from our vantage point today. In **Chapter 4: Is the Church Asleep?**, we'll address this topic by surveying the church's response to the issue of race through various periods of American history: slavery, post-slavery, the Civil Rights era, and the modern era. This is an essential part of the journey to wokeness—and to understanding the plight of our family members who are people of color.

We'll talk in **Chapter 5** about **Things for the Church to Lament**. Woke minds require sober thinking, and sober thinking leads us to lament sin's devastation. The concept of lament is not popular. We're not comfortable with it. We like to rush quickly to our praises and hallelujahs. But God's Word encourages and allows us to take time to grieve. I'll share ten things that I lament regarding where we are today as the church.

Be Accountable. Where there has been silence in the past, we now have the awesome opportunity to reclaim our roles as light and salt in our world. We need to be known for speaking the truth to one another in love so that we can deal effectively with the problems of race and injustice in the church and in the world. In doing so, we become an effective gospel community with a ferocious prophetic voice. The call to be a Woke Church requires us to reclaim our biblical identity as the people of God.

In **Chapter 6: Reclaiming Our Prophetic Voice**, we will outline seven crucial components of prophetic preaching. Prophetic preaching must: contain the gospel, be centered on Jesus, be clear on the issues, be biblically informed, be rhetorically contending, provide visionary hope, and offer clear statements of action. We will be encouraged to see the church as a prophetic community. The reader will be encouraged to no longer be silent on injustice in our culture.

Chapter 7: A Vision for Change will present the framework for how the Woke Church should think about its approach to justice. I'll suggest that we should have a three-level approach to justice: 1) Intervening Justice: the effort to tend to and meet pressing needs without which persons will not be receptive to the gospel message; 2) Preventative Justice: taking a proactive approach to issues of justice to get ahead of and stem the tide of the evils that challenge our communities; and 3) Systemic Justice: developing programmatic approaches to address systems that have historically worked against the principles of justice.

Be Active. Ephesians 5:16 says, "*making the most of the time,* because the days are evil." The KJV says, "*Redeeming the time,* because the days are evil." Making the most of the time, or redeeming the time, is the word *exagorazomai*, which means "to do something with intensity and urgency . . . to take full advantage of every opportunity."[8]

At its best, this concept challenges us to maximize the opportunity for the gospel. Race, justice, and dignity are huge issues for gospel common ground. When Christians spend time arguing about what's going on in the public square and not engaging it, we miss redemptive opportunities.

One of our church planters had a basketball court in the neighborhood that was in shambles. The pastor of the church, Doug Logan, got with several churches (white and multiethnic churches), and they worked together with the city to restore the courts. City leaders were so impressed that they began to provide materials and paid their workers overtime to help with clean-up because they were so shocked that a church cared. Because of this and many other activities, the mayor and the pastor built a viable relationship. The neighborhood was blown away and granted the pastor a street nickname: "Pastor Diddy." He became a part of their village, and he and the church are able to engage the neighborhood with a free "hood pass." A hood pass is when the residents and the thugs put the word out that no one is to bother the pass holder, or there will be consequences. Now Logan is the go-to guy for funerals in the neighborhood where he is able to proclaim freely the gospel and lead people to Jesus.

In this section, we'll talk about ways the church can actively engage the issue of justice in our communities.

Chapter 8: The Woke Church in Action will suggest ten action steps that the church can engage in to bring healing and justice into our spheres. Among them is the concept of making *Imago Dei* a part of the foundational biblical and gospel education for all believers. Just as the Jerusalem Council clarified issues that were to be foundational Christian practices for Gentiles, so the Western church needs the valuing of people as created in the image of God as a key part of its teaching. We'll discuss the Woke Church Think Tank and consider what it looks like when believers join swords to fight this battle together.

In **Chapter 9: Seeing Through the Lens of the End**, we'll be reminded of the blessed hope that the future holds for every believer. It is impossible to talk about race and injustice without having in mind as a believer what the future holds for the church. Revelation 7:9–17 gives us a picture of what is to come. There is a revolution coming. The universal church will stand before the eternal God and praise the Son. And in that eternity, all ethnicities will be distinct yet unified because of Jesus Christ. That will be glory!

I love the church. I love the fact that we get to be a part of the called-out Body of Christ in the world right now. Right in the middle of all that is wrong with our world. That's a privilege. But I do believe that the church should already be woke. We should already be champions for justice. We have a gospel imperative that challenges us to care for the least among us. Like my son Nehemiah, there's a part of me, deep down inside, that's almost inconsolable when I think of the great divide in the family of believers in this country. It's from that place of deep pain and struggle that I appeal to you to share this journey with me. Let's wake up, church. Let's get at it.

HOW BIG IS THE GOSPEL? (JUSTICE AND THE GOSPEL)

I grew up in a Christian home. I was a church boy but not a Christian. At Brightwood Park United Methodist Church on the corner of 9th and Jefferson Streets in northwest Washington, D.C., I found a haven. The black church for me was a refuge from the crack-infested streets that riddled my neighborhood. It was one of the central places of help and aid for us. It was where I got a chance at my first public singing solo; my first opportunities to lead. I heard the liturgy and the songs of Zion and the Word preached, but I wasn't a believer. In this environment, however, I had the seeds of the gospel planted in me as well as the nurturing of my dignity as a human. I'm forever grateful for this.

After I graduated from Archbishop Carroll High School, I went to Bowie State University (one of the oldest historically black colleges in the country). While on the campus I began to learn about my African heritage. I soon began to reject Christianity and became hostile toward the faith. I started drinking and smoking weed. But I always felt out of place—like there was some type of call pulling me and challenging me about my current condition. One day I decided to go to the campus ministry worship service with a young lady I was dating. While there, I heard the gospel of Jesus just as clear as I can see the words I'm writing now. I placed my confidence in the finished work of Jesus Christ on the cross and the resurrection as a propitiation for my sins.

For about nine months, I wrestled as an undiscipled, new believer. A young man from a theologically charismatic background began to disciple my roommate and me. As I began to grow, I started to shed things in my life that were sins and encumbrances (Heb. 12:1–3), and I began the discipline of fixing my eyes on Jesus, the Author and Perfecter of my faith. As I grew, it was clear to me that I was called to minister. During this time, I started courting my beautiful wife, Yvette. She took me to her home church, First Baptist Church of Highland Park in Landover, Maryland. There I heard the glorious gospel every Sunday under the leadership of Rev. Dr. James J. McCord.

The gospel that saved my soul in 1992 gave me a new heart— one that was knit together with Christ and knit together with my Christian brothers and sisters. It compels me to seek what is good and what is right for my fellow man.

WHAT IS THE GOSPEL?

The apostle Paul in writing to the Corinthians clarifies the essence of the gospel:

> For what I received I passed on to you as of first importance: that Christ died for our sins according to the

Scriptures, that he was buried, that he was raised on the third day according to the Scriptures, and that he appeared to Cephas, and then to the Twelve. After that, he appeared to more than five hundred of the brothers and sisters at the same time, most of whom are still living, though some have fallen asleep. (1 Cor. 15:3–6 NIV)

In his declaration of the gospel as "of first importance," Paul is clarifying that these truths are central for salvation. He reiterates this crucial message to the believers at Colossae:

Once you were alienated from God and were enemies in your minds because of your evil behavior. But now he has reconciled you by Christ's physical body through death to present you holy in his sight, without blemish and free from accusation—if you continue in your faith, established and firm, and do not move from the hope held out in the gospel. This is the gospel that you heard and that has been proclaimed to every creature under heaven, and of which I, Paul, have become a servant. (Col. 1:21–23 NIV)

THE GOSPEL AND RECONCILIATION

This is the glorious gospel! We have been reconciled to God by the death of Jesus Christ. We rejoice in that truth. But in the gospel, man is not just reconciled to God by faith. Man is also reconciled to man by faith. (See 2 Cor. 5:18). God has given to us the ministry of reconciliation. He doesn't give us the luxury of refusing to be reconciled. If God could pursue reconciliation with us—in spite of all of our sins, our rebellion, our issues—we should be rushing toward one another to reconcile.

I remember when God was challenging me about people that I needed to straighten things out with. And I didn't like it. It seemed like God challenged me: "I need you to go handle it." I'm honest with God without being disrespectful, so I said, "I'm not really feeling like working it out." God challenged me again with something like "I don't care what you feel like. So, until you move toward reconciliation, I'm going to lean on you. I'm going to lean up against your soul until you're uncomfortable." That's how you know you're a Christian. You know you're a Christian when God seems to say, "I'm going to put you into this terrifying submission hold." I'm not talking about in the flesh. I'm talking about in the spirit. When you get hit in the soul, it's ten times more terrifying than being hit in the flesh.

It was as if He put me into a headlock and began tightening His grip. And when I continued to resist, He was like, "Well, I'm going to tighten it up." What's funny is that you try to run, and your running just makes it worse. So you try to surf the web, try to go shopping, try to have fun. And you can't have fun because the Holy Ghost just will not let you go. And finally you surrender.

I remember trying to set up this reconciliation meeting. And I was frustrated with the whole situation. But I was pursuing and doing all that I needed to do on my end. I sensed God challenging me again: "When you go in there, it's not about other people. It's about you obeying Me. Don't worry about the response. You go in, and you obey Me." I'm like, "Okay, I'm going to be obedient." So I went in. I sought reconciliation. I wrestled and fought against my flesh. Reconciliation didn't happen. But the headlock ended because from God's perspective, I had done what He commanded me to do. I wasn't responsible for how the other person responded.

That's why the Bible says, "If it is possible, as far as it depends on you, live at peace with everyone" (Rom. 12:18 NIV). There's no peace like God-sent peace. And this is what should mark us as the people and the family of God. We are the sheepfold, the body, the new humanity, chosen race, new creation, the elect, exiles, royal priesthood, living stones, and temple of the living God! All of this speaks not of our individuality, but of our connectivity through Jesus' death by faith. Since this is true, we must pursue honest reconciliation that faces the issues of our broken past in this country. We must take time to revisit our history and proclaim the gospel to each season and seek reconciliation, restoration, and restitution, as it is appropriate.

This is the gospel mandate. And we dare not truncate it or reduce it to one of its parts. The danger of reductionism is that it attempts to focus on a single aspect to the neglect of others. That is not the goal of this book. The goal of this book is to shine a spotlight on one of the aspects of the gospel that has been neglected and dismissed as inappropriate for discourse.

The gospel has far-reaching implications. I remember having to use several remotes for everything. There was a remote for the VCR, a remote for the TV, a remote for the cable, a remote for the DVD, and another one for the stereo. But someone had a smart idea. They took one remote and used it to program all of those receivers to respond to it. They called it the all-in-one. All-in-one meant that all your electronic devices could be activated by one remote that had it all. I believe that the gospel is an all-in-one remote for salvation and living the Christian life. We are saved by the gospel, and we live out the gospel in every facet of our lives.

The chart on the following page illustrates how the gospel is to saturate the life of the believer. It shows how a woke believer is to impact home, community, and, ultimately, the world for Christ.

Pastor Tony Evans describes the debate in Christian circles about how the gospel and justice should relate to one another.

There is some confusion today about the implications of the gospel, and to what degree the gospel includes this mandate of justice. Some Christians believe that to include social liberation and justice in the gospel is to preach a "different gospel." Others believe that to exclude social liberation and justice as part of the gospel is to deny the gospel.[1]

Gospel Saturation

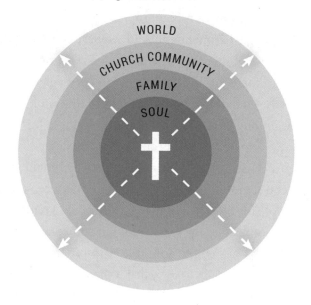

WORLD

CHURCH COMMUNITY

FAMILY

SOUL

THE GOSPEL AND JUSTICE

When I think about the sinfulness of man, I'm keenly aware that it would have been just and fair for God to leave us eternally separated from Him (Rev. 20). Yet, God mercifully created a way to save me from being a violator of His just law (Gal. 3:13)! Jesus became my just representative and died under unjust circumstances (2 Cor. 5:21). God used the injustice of Rome and the Jews as a means for Jesus, the innocent, to take on my guilt and legally pay for my sin (Luke 9:22). He paid for my sin by being my propitiation (1 John 2:2).

> Although justification is a work of God's grace ("[they] are justified freely by his grace," v. 24), it is nevertheless not at the expense of his justice—understanding by justice God's rectitude, that attribute by means of which he does all things justly and rightly. There is no conflict in our justification between God's justice and his grace, since both meet at the cross of Christ. God provides the sacrifice (by grace) and Christ bears the penalty for our sins (satisfying God's justice).[2]

We have to be careful about placing limitations on the attributes of God. In Western theology, we tend to lack a comprehensive view of God's perfections, particularly righteousness/justice and even our understanding of justification. Justification is a huge greenhouse of truth that extends beyond "being declared righteous"! Justified isn't merely a position, but a practice! Christ's righteousness being imputed to us by faith leads to our being made right with God as well as our making things right on earth—knowing that Jesus will return and bring to completion the work that He has been doing through His people.

> There are few words in any language that can equal *dikaiosis* for theological depth and resonance. It has been at the center of scholarly debate for centuries. Known largely as "justification," it is still a key word in ecumenical discussion. Yet we have great difficulty in translating it into English. We need to absorb the teaching of Austin Farrer, who wrote, "God has no attitudes which are not actions; the two things are one."[3]

In essence, we tend to have a one-dimensional understanding of justification. It is important to view the Romans 5–6 and the 2 Corinthians 5 sense of righteousness as both intrinsic and extrinsic. In other words, it is an attribute and an action. The following quote by Fleming Rutledge expands upon this idea:

> When a reader of the Bible discovers that the verb translated "justify" and the nouns "justification," "righteousness," and "justice" are the same word, the effect on that reader's understanding can be revolutionary. Ernst Käsemann opened up a new understanding of the term *dikaiosis*, traditionally translated "justification," that continues to bear fruit into the twenty-first century. In his groundbreaking essay "The Righteousness of God in Paul," he shows that God's *dikaiosyne* is not an attribute but a power, namely, "a power that brings salvation to pass." Thus, "righteousness" does not mean moral perfection. It is not a distant, forbidding characteristic of God that humans are supposed to try to emulate or imitate; there is no good news in that. Instead, the righteousness of God is God's powerful activity of making right what is wrong in the world. When we read, in both Old and New Testaments, that God is righteous, we are to understand that God is at work in his creation doing right. He is overcoming evil, delivering the oppressed, raising the poor from the dust, vindicating the voiceless victims who have had no one to defend them.[4]

The way we are taught about these aspects of the gospel deeply affects our understanding and the way we process justice. When we have a reductionist understanding of justification, we fail to see the holistic picture of the gospel. God's righteousness is Him making all things right. As disciples of Jesus, we are being made right and fighting with humility as we announce the kingdom. Again, as Paul writes in Titus 3:1–14, he shows both gospel ethics and gospel ethos. Regeneration is a motivation for good works. It is a fruit of gospel transformation. Paul calls God the Father a philanthropist *(Philanthropia)*. In other words, His philanthropy is both transformative to the soul and expressed by His action upon us. He expects us to be active in good works for His glory as a response and proof that we have been transformed. As Jesus stated to His disciples in John 15:8: "My Father is glorified by this: that you produce much fruit and prove to be my disciples."

In light of this glorious truth, we are to proclaim the gospel to change people within systems. It is important for us not to disconnect the gospel from the Kingdom. In proclaiming the gospel, we are to proclaim the reality of an already and not yet kingdom. In Mark 1:14–15, we find Jesus doing just this. After John was arrested, Jesus went to Galilee, proclaiming the good news of God: "The time is fulfilled, and the kingdom of God has come near. Repent and believe the good news!"

J. Dwight Pentecost used to speak of the kingdom as being near: "the kingdom is within your grasp." What Jesus did was show that the good news touches every area of life. Being transformed by the gospel means that we as the covenant community bring that newness of life wherever we go. Our desire should be for our kingdom activity to point to the need for the soul to be changed.

THE BIBLE AND JUSTICE

It's concerning to me when I take note of the themes that are emphasized as central to the Bible, and see that justice is rarely mentioned. We rightly believe that Jesus is central (John 5:37, Luke 24:27); the glory of God is central (Eph. 1); and the gospel is central in all of its parts: creation, fall, redemption, and consummation (Rom. 1:20; 5:18–21; 10:9–13; 8:18–30). But I don't believe that we spend nearly as much time on justice as a major theme of the Bible. This is crucial because it has direct application to the issues of race and injustice in this country.

Jesus invites us to look at all of Scripture through the lens of justice. He tells the Pharisees that in all their work to understand Yahweh, they have missed this key element of justice.

> Woe to you, scribes and Pharisees, hypocrites! You pay a tenth of mint, dill, and cumin, and yet you have neglected the more important matters of the law—justice, mercy, and faithfulness. These things should have been done without neglecting the others. (Matt. 23:23)

Jesus is talking to the scribes and the leaders because their role was to lead God's people toward the kingdom and to help them develop a heart for God and toward Jesus. But instead of doing that, they weighed them down with trivial requirements and squabbles that didn't help them see Jesus more clearly, nor did it help them be salt and light to the lost. The Lord Jesus calls justice a weighty matter in Scripture. Jesus is using a play on words by contrasting the naturally light weight of the mint, dill, and cumin with the weight and expanse of deeper matters of the law. According to R. T. France, "There is no suggestion that the scribes and Pharisees were opposed in principle to justice, mercy, and faithfulness. The problem was that they did not devote the same care to working out the practical implications of these basic principles as they did to the minutiae of tithing herbs."[5]

What minutiae are we engaging in to show our dedication to exegesis, historical theology, biblical theology, systematic theology, Old Testament, New Testament, Bible exposition, hermeneutics, pastoral theology, etc. while we miss some of the key opportunities for fleshing out and communicating a commitment to the heart of God? What minutiae do we need to reprioritize in order that we might get to many of the core commitments that Jesus wants us to focus on in and through the church? I'm not suggesting that we neglect proper exegesis and hermeneutics, but that we must prioritize our call to serve the needs of justice. Let's turn the tide and become the beastly gospel community that God wants us to be as the Woke Church. Since the gospel has awakened us, we need to walk in that comprehensive awakening without neglecting all the other things that the Lord requires of us.

JUSTICE AS A HUGE THEME IN THE BIBLE

I love the picture in Proverbs 31 of the queen mother who is teaching her son who would someday be king: "Speak up for those who cannot speak for themselves, for the rights of all who are destitute. Speak up and judge fairly; defend the rights of the poor and needy" (Prov. 31:8–9 NIV). It's interesting how this queen demonstrates wisdom as she delivers one of the greatest leadership lessons in history—to a soon-to-be monarch.

So this mother is teaching a variety of lessons to this son. She says, "Son, you're going to be king one day."

He's probably ignoring her, because he's a prince now. He's ready to get his kingdom. He's been watching Pops and is probably already thinking, *Pops, move out of the way. I'm ready to wreck shop as king.*

But the queen mother acts as the character of his kingliness. And what she does is tell him several things. She says, "Son, when you get in power, the women who don't like you right now, they're gonna like you then. You're gonna have to fall back from them. I'm going to tell you a little later how to choose a wife because with all that stuff coming at you, son, you're going to have to know how to pick a wife." Now, that's a good mother right there.

However, what's interesting is that neatly nestled in there is her advice on how to use his power. She starts talking to him about justice. This is so important because the natural tendency of one in leadership and privilege is not to use their privilege and their power on behalf of others. And so she tells him, "This is what you're going to have to do. There are going to be aristocrats and those who are in power that are going to try to influence your kingliness to use it for themselves. They'll try to make you denigrate those who don't have a voice. Therefore, I want you to look beyond the foolishness of those who are in the aristocratic positions, who try to keep everything for themselves and try to press down on people that don't have a voice and are not like them, press down on people that they can use to continue their legacy of privilege and wealth."

This mother challenges this would-be king with how he should respond in the face of injustice: "Open your mouth for the mute. For the rights of all who are destitute." She says something beautiful, particularly in the second verse, "Open your mouth. Judge righteously." Now what's interesting here is that this mother may not realize it, but she is a theologian. And she's using the two-sided coin of justice and righteousness. The same word (*tsedeq*, Hebrew; *dikaios*, Greek) is used for justice and righteousness. Justice points to extrinsic execution of the heart of God, and righteousness means intrinsic impact by the heart of God.

You have to be intrinsically changed by God in order for justice to be done. In other words, justice doesn't come by legislation, because you can legislate things and nothing changes. We can go to the executive branch. We can go to the legislative branch. We can go to the judicial branch. We can put whatever kind of Supreme Court justices we want to put in place. But at the end of the day legislation doesn't change hearts . . . only the gospel does.

Do we continue to press for legislation? Yes! Do we press for systemic change? Yes! Do we maximize the advantages of being born in America? Yes. We have some founding documents that have never been fulfilled. So we must continue to work together to hold America accountable for what it promised to do. But we understand that we have at our disposal something that is much greater than man-made documents. We have the glorious gospel!

Unfortunately, today justice seems to be seen as a "liberal" word, not a word that pervades the Scripture. Thankfully, many of us are waking up to the recognition that justice is a core message of the Bible. The Bible is filled with justice as a main theme. It shouts from the blood of righteous Abel to the establishment of the eternal Kingdom of God.

We will engage briefly the source and practice of justice for the church. Here are some passages on the matter throughout the Old Testament.

> "You must not deny justice to a poor person among you in his lawsuit." (Ex. 23:6)

> "Pursue justice and justice alone, so that you will live and possess the land the LORD your God is giving you." (Deut. 16:20)

> "Do not act unjustly when deciding a case. Do not be partial to the poor or give preference to the rich; judge your neighbor fairly." (Lev. 19:15)

> So David reigned over all Israel, administering justice and righteousness for all his people. (2 Sam. 8:15)

> "Blessed be the LORD your God! He delighted in you and put you on the throne of Israel, because of the

LORD's eternal love for Israel. He has made you king to carry out justice and righteousness." (1 Kings 10:9)

The king consulted the wise men who understood the times, for it was his normal procedure to confer with experts in law and justice. (Est. 1:13)

He loves righteousness and justice;
the earth is full of the LORD's unfailing love. (Ps. 33:5)

But you must return to your God.
Maintain love and justice,
and always put your hope in God. (Hos. 12:6)

But let justice flow like water,
and righteousness, like an unfailing stream. (Amos 5:24)

Because I have sinned against him,
I must endure the Lord's rage
until he champions my cause
and establishes justice for me.
He will bring me into the light;
I will see his salvation. (Mic. 7:9)

He applies his justice morning by morning;
he does not fail at dawn. (Zeph. 3:5)

There are countless other verses for future study: 1 Sam. 8:3; 1 Chron. 18:14; 2 Chron. 9:8; Job 36:6; Prov. 29:4; Eccl. 3:15; Isa. 1:17; Jer. 5:5; Lam. 3:35; Ezek. 34:16; Hab. 1:7. More than half of the books in the Old Testament speak of justice as an attribute of God and a responsibility of His people.

JUSTICE IN GOD'S CHARACTER

We can't know God without understanding His heart for justice. From the beginning God revealed Himself as a just God. When Adam and Eve sinned in the Garden of Eden, it was God's justice that required the first shedding of blood to provide a covering for their nakedness. It was His justice on display that sent them away from the garden forever with the promise of One who would bruise the head of the serpent (Gen. 3:15).

The early church father Tertullian, in responding to people who suggested that his concern for justice meant that he was not being faithful to the gospel, said this:

> from the very first the Creator was both good and also just. And both His attributes advanced together. His goodness created; His justice arranged, the world; and in this process it even then decreed that the world should be formed of good materials, because it took counsel with goodness. The work of justice is apparent, in the separation which was pronounced between light and darkness, between day and night, between heaven and earth, between the water above and the water beneath.[6]

Tertullian asserted that justice was on display in and through creation. God applied justice in how He separated one aspect of creation from the other.

The prophet Daniel declares that God is righteous or just when He punishes His people for their disobedience (Dan. 9:14). In saying this, Daniel is stressing the fact that God's character is just. He is a just God. He is the source of all true justice. Justice is sometimes taken together with the righteousness of God. The justice of God means that God is entirely correct and just in all His dealings with humanity; moreover, this justice acts in accordance with His law. In other words, to say that God is just means that God isn't confused about what is right. Rightness is who He is at all times. This rightness makes its way to the home of every believer because His primary expectation is justice and rightness on the part of all that He has created—especially those who are in covenant with Him! God's covenant community is the purveyor of His character in all of life.

Seeing God in this way helps define and root justice in the Lord. To ignore justice is to ignore God. Justice isn't God (we don't worship justice), but His justice is one of His key attributes. This means that God's justice has practical connection to our everyday lives. We have the ability to experience it. We see God's justice personified in Jesus. He will return and restore justice, by judging the seen and unseen kings of the earth and those evil forces that motivated the wickedness of their kingdoms as well as rewarding the righteous for obeying the gospel (2 Thess. 1:8; Rev. 20–22).

We are called to share in God's justice as His image bearers. He expects justice to be exacted and for us to be His representatives of justice in this world. We will all be called into account for how we reflected His character in justice. How did we discipline our children? What was our work ethic? How did we treat employees? Did we speak out against injustice? Did we act justly?

JUSTICE AS THE CHARACTER OF THE CHURCH

Jesus' feeding the five thousand was about authentic care for the hunger of the crowd, but He also wanted to creatively engage their hunger in a way that transcended their need for physical food. Luke and John both show us that Jesus cared for the crowd, both physically and spiritually! He fed them (Luke 9:13–17); He preached the kingdom to them and did works that pointed to the eternal kingdom He would one day bring (v. 11); and He presented

Himself as the true bread of life (vv. 22–59). We are called to follow His example of caring for the physical needs of others in order that the gospel witness of the kingdom might saturate the earth.

What would it look like for the church to mirror Christ's pattern of meeting physical needs in order to have access to the hearts of men and women? The early church got it right. Acts 2 shares the story of how they gave themselves to the teaching of the apostles, and whenever they discovered that someone had a need, they would sell some of their possessions and distribute the proceeds to care for the need. And God responded by "[adding] to the church daily such as should be saved" (KJV).

Doing inner-city work keeps my eyes open to the justice gaps daily. I see fatherlessness, violence literally on our front steps, educational challenges, gentrification, redlining, and the poor having very little access to healthy food options, which impact education and mortality. These realities could be daunting without all of the riches that heaven brings us through Jesus. I love to walk and ride my bike through the neighborhood of Epiphany and meet people. It's been good to see what's going on, share the gospel, and just dream of the kingdom coming to the neighborhood. As difficult as it is sometimes to witness the brokenness, I find hope in what only Jesus can do through the church.

As exiles in this world, we must see ourselves as incarnational missionaries in the world for justice. Shalom is the means for justice to be done. Jesus said, "Blessed are the peacemakers, for they will be called children of God" (Matt. 5:9 NIV). Since we are children of God, we must be peacemakers. We can't be peacemakers and ignore injustice. Ignoring injustice isn't a sign of being an authentic believer. Particularly, ignoring systemic injustice. Even Israel in its exile in Babylon was called to be a kingdom people who sought the peace and prosperity of the city (Jer. 29:7). Although this is specific to the exile of Israel, Jesus and the apostles pick up the exilic theme of our being strangers who are peacemakers. Consider this quote from Lois Barrett in *Missional Church*:

> Shalom envisions the full prosperity of a people of God living under the covenant of God's demanding care and compassionate rule. In the prophetic vision, peace such as this comes hand in hand with justice. Without justice, there can be no real peace, and without peace, no real justice. Indeed, only in a social world full of a peace grounded in justice can there come the full expression of joy and celebration.[7]

God's shalom is God's divine work of re-stitching broken creation to His purpose and design. Timothy Keller defines the biblical concept of *shalom* as universal flourishing, wholeness, and delight: "God created the world to be a fabric, for everything to be woven together and interdependent."[8] I love this picture of the church as "woven together and interdependent." It suggests that we need one another. We can't image Christ to a watching world apart from each other.

The American philosopher Nicholas Wolterstorff says:

> Shalom is the human being dwelling at peace in all his or her relationships with God, with self, with fellows, with nature. . . . But the peace which is shalom is not merely the absence of hostility, not merely being in right relationship. Shalom at its highest is enjoyment in one's relationships. . . . Shalom in the first place incorporates right, harmonious relationships to God and delight in service. . . . Secondly, shalom incorporates right harmonious relationships to other human beings and delight in human community. . . . thirdly, shalom

incorporates right, harmonious relationships to nature
and delight in our physical surroundings. . . . Justice, the
enjoyment of one's rights, is indispensable to shalom.
[Therefore] justice is wounded when shalom is absent.[9]

As incarnational missionaries, our mission flows from the
mission of the gospel of practicing peace. As the church, we are
called to be peace practitioners. In the words of Darrell Guder,
"By incarnational mission, I mean the understanding and practice of Christian witness that is rooted in and shaped by the life,
ministry, suffering, death, and resurrection of Jesus"—the gospel.[10] As we walk as a Holy Spirit community, we are empowered by His divine presence to fight for peace in multiple layers
of society. Our witness depends on our commitment to showing
off the glory of Jesus in how we work in the world to be agents
of change. Being agents of change means speaking to its brokenness, but also having the skill to use the truth to serve in bringing
solutions. We have the vision and strategic acumen of Joseph.
The ability to see the problem and formulate viable solutions is
our vocation.

This reality may call on us to broaden our understanding of
missional community. Those times on Wednesday and Thursday
night, those are just missional community rallies. You're supposed to gather and then to scatter. Missional community is not
just when you gather. You're still a missional community when
you're in the city. That means when you go get your ramen noo-
dles at Whole Foods or Trader Joe's. Whenever you're there,
you're supposed to be opening up your life so God can give you
common ground with people who are not like you. This is where
we live out the gospel. The gospel is supposed to bring people together who wouldn't naturally be together. That's the nature of it.

I agree with Justin Martyr, the early Christian apologist: "We used to hate and destroy one another and refused to associate with people of another race or country. Now, because of Christ, we live together with such people and pray for our enemies."[11]

This is what the gospel does. It causes those who used to be enemies to now become friends.

We desperately need the gospel. I need the gospel. Every day I need Jesus' gospel to shepherd my heart and mind. When I see all the bad news on my newsfeed on Facebook, if I'm not in my Bible, preaching the gospel to myself, looking at the eschatological hope, I will lose my mind. And so I'm glad that when we see the injustices and the brokenness of our society we have the tool of God's Word to help us become change agents—to make a difference in our spheres of influence. The gospel is the truth that unites us. It is the common ground that knits our souls together as one.

How big is the gospel? I believe in a gospel that is big enough to root out indifference, apathy, ignorance, and poverty of soul. It's big enough to change utterly lost men and women into bold champions of the faith. It's big enough to wake a slumbering church from its sleep. It's a gospel that cries out for a Woke Church.

WE'RE FAMILY, WE'RE HOLY

I remember accepting my first pastoral position at Good Hope Missionary Baptist Church in Houston, Texas. It is one of the oldest black churches in Houston. I can remember teaching the Wednesday noonday Bible study for the older saints. I was twenty-six years old, and they were all between 75 and 95 years of age. I had learned Hebrew, Greek, and was learning Aramaic. I was trying to teach them theology and all about the hypostatic union. I thought I was doing something. But you know what they did for me? They didn't wrestle me down and tell me to stop being arrogant. They said, "Baby, you're gonna have to break that down for us." And here's what they did. They cooked me bread pudding and real gumbo. When my wife was sick, they took care of us. We were far from home, and they invited us into their home for Thanksgiving. Over that period of time, the church was patient with me. They showed me what true family looks like.

Family loves on one another. Family takes care of one another. Family is patient with one another.

If I'm honest, there are times when I don't want to be patient with some of my siblings who struggle to get it when we talk about these issues of racism and justice. It's hard for me to hear the constant refrain of "just preach the gospel." When the topic is abortion, nobody says, "just preach the gospel." We preach against abortion as if it's a gospel issue. When the topic is sex trafficking, no one says "just preach the gospel." We develop a battalion to go and get people out of sex trafficking. And we *should* because these are crucial issues. But so is racial justice!

Much of my zeal and anger around the issue of justice comes from impatience with those who know very well what Scripture teaches, but choose to apply it selectively. When my impatience threatens to boil over, I remember those beautiful saints at Good Hope who gently nudged and nurtured me through my season of arrogance and pride. I ask God to help me freely give to others what I have received.

Every blood-washed child of God is part of the family of God. Family is where you receive your greatest encouragements and also your greatest hurts. Family is where we learn dignity, significance, purpose, and our value. It's the place we feel accepted and get a sense of belonging.

WE'RE FAMILY

I love how the apostle Paul dealt with this aspect of family across ethnic lines when he wrote to Philemon. He addressed the letter to Philemon and others, including "the church that meets in [his] house." Philemon was a slave owner, and the church met in his home. For the church to meet in someone's house meant that they were a big deal. A total baller. They had a middle courtyard that was open and they would have gatherings there. They likely had slaves serving at the gatherings.

Philemon's name means "affectionate one.'" So just by addressing him by his name, Paul was calling him to live up to his name.
Paul says to Philemon, "I always thank my God when I mention
you in my prayers" (Philem. 4). I struggle with this. Paul was mistaken for an Egyptian, so he clearly was not white (Acts 21:38). He
would have surely been aware of the Egyptian caste system, the
Damascus caste system, and the Roman caste system. How could
Paul say to a believer who holds slaves, "I'm praying for you"? As
a matter of fact, he says, "you come up in my prayers a whole lot."

What he's saying is really convicting to me. As much as I may
want to give up on evangelicalism, I cannot give up on Jesus and
the church. I must affectionately pray for the family of God, the
body of Christ. Those who love me, and those who despise me.
As broken as we are, and as separate and splintered and filled
with schisms, we are siblings. We are called Christians, followers
of Christ. That's a high calling to live up to, isn't it? Our name
requires us to live like Christ because we're family.

Paul encourages and challenges Philemon: "Because I hear of
your love and faith toward the Lord Jesus and for all the saints"
(Philem. 5). Then he begins to make it more specific: "I pray that
your participation in the faith may become effective through
knowing." This knowing (*epignosko*) is knowledge that comes from
experience. It's not just information. It's a holistic knowledge made
possible by an experience. He's challenging Philemon to make his
"love for all the saints" real by participating with different believers, in different economic classes, from different ethnicities. And
he's getting ready to give Philemon an experiment that will help
him understand what this "love for the saints" is all about.

That test involves how he responds to Onesimus, a slave who
he owned and who had escaped from him. In God's providence,
this escaped slave met Paul and came to faith in Christ. Paul had
specific instructions for both of these men that are powerful

help to us as we ponder how to start acting like family. Paul challenges both of them to move toward one another, not away from one another.

Onesimus is faced with the question of whether he will accept Paul's challenge to return to his former slave master. It's hard to imagine how frightening the thought of returning to a slave master that he had escaped from must have been. His dilemma raises the question of whether we are pastorable or not. Being pastorable means that if I'm confronted with what God wants me to do, I may be angry. Yet, when the dust of my soul's anger settles, I accept the fact that God—because He is God and because He is my Father—has the right to command me to do things that don't feel good . . . that I would never choose to do on my own. And because in this family God is the Father, I choose to obey. Onesimus did that. He willed himself to return to Philemon in obedience to Paul's instructions.

Paul prepared Philemon for his former slave's return by referring to Onesimus as his "son" and his "very own heart." I love that! Being in the family of God elevates your status from "slave" to son and brother. But this is what blows my mind. Paul says to Philemon, "perhaps this is why he was separated from you for a brief time" (v. 15). The word "separated" here is a word for sovereignty. It's a word that means that God sovereignly separated Philemon and Onesimus for a divine purpose beyond both of them. He's saying, "I believe Onesimus was separated from you for God to do more in your separation than He could do with you together."

Here's a question: What if God sovereignly allowed the church to be racially separate for a time because He intends to impact the world by bringing us all together as one family? What if the things that are happening right now in our country are God's way of telling us it's time to wake up and act like family?

Paul is saying three things to Philemon: 1) don't beat Onesimus when he comes back; 2) treat him like your family; and 3) commission him as a missionary and send him back to me. That's wild! That's revolutionary. Paul is deconstructing an unjust system through Philemon. He's saying you have no eternal legal right to beat your brother. Jesus said, "as you did it to one of the least of these my brothers, you did it to me" (Matt. 25:40 ESV). Second, he's family and that means now you have an unbreakable, eternal bond with him. But not only that, Paul is saying, "I know you'll do more, because I did ask you for a favor, didn't I? I said send him back to me. So I'm trusting that you're going to gather the church in your home and in front of everyone you are going to commission him as a gospel missionary."

We can't miss what Paul is doing. Paul is calling on Philemon—in front of everybody—to exalt Onesimus, his former slave, as a spiritual sibling and co-laborer in the gospel! You know that word would have traveled. What would that do to the other slaves that were under Philemon's care? Do you think they would be content? They would all be getting saved!

And what would that have done to Philemon's friends? There would be a lot of conversation over wine, tea, and coffee, where he's sitting down and hearing, "You let him do *what*? Who *does* that? Who has slaves that run away and come back and you reward him? Where does that come from?" Philemon could say, "I'm glad you asked. God has been dealing with my heart about slavery." "Dealing with your heart? What about your pockets?" "No, man. If I lose, I lose, but God is able to reward even when you give stuff away. Not only did I send him away; he had to get there. He was broke, so I had to give him some resources so he could get there. We took up a church offering for him." And his friends would have to be thinking, *This is weird. I need to meditate on this.* Now, that's how you change a system. You change a system by converting the poor and the elite at the same time.

I love how Paul closes out his letter to Philemon. He signs off by listing those who he is partnering with to do ministry. There was Epaphroditus, a Colossian; Mark, a north African Jew, a nephew of Barnabas; Aristarchus, who was a Macedonian Jew; Demas, and Luke, the Antiochan physician who was a Gentile (v. 23–24). We see this multiethnic, multicolored group of people that do gospel ministry together. And they are a family.

Ultimately we were all runaways, prodigals who, through Jesus Christ, God brought us into relationship with Him. God, through the gospel, brought us in and made us family. God is our Father and Jesus is our elder brother. We're brothers and sisters. We're family.

WE'RE HOLY

We're family. But we're also a special *kind* of family. We're not just any kind of family. We're to be holy. When God established Israel as His chosen people, He let them know that their witness was meant to be a display of God's holiness to one another and to the world. He tells them to be holy because He is holy. "And the LORD spoke to Moses, saying, 'Speak to all the congregation of the people of Israel and say to them, You shall be holy, for I the LORD your God am holy'" (Lev. 19:1–2 ESV). We must start here. We can't start with pragmatic stuff. We have to start off with who God is and who we are. What we do flows out of who we are in Him. If we don't start with who we are in the living God, we are no more than social activists and speakers without any power or any strength for long-term systemic change. What makes us different is the Lord God Yahweh being in our lives as the promoter and the strengthener who empowers everything that we do.

It's interesting to me that God starts out with holiness as

a description of the character for His people. The word holiness means "to cut." In other words, to cut something off from something that it was originally connected to in order to give it uniqueness. Even though it may have some similarities to what it was cut away from, it is no longer connected to what it was cut away from.

It reminds me of something that my sons in the ministry did for me a few years ago. For our ten-year anniversary, they gave me a gift and told me to do something for myself that I would not ordinarily do. So I went to a tailor and had something made. I went in there and picked out the fabric, and they measured me (*I was bigger than I thought I was*). When a tailor begins, he starts with a big roll of fabric. Based on the amount of fabric that's needed for the garment, they cut that away from the large roll of fabric. When they cut that away, it is no longer assigned to what it was connected to. Its assignment has changed to being a part of what the tailor needs for his purposes. In other words, the church of God was a part of the ream of the world, and when the Lord God came and pulled us out, He cut us away from what we were. And now the Church of God through Jesus Christ is uniquely tailored to wear kingdom garments. We're uniquely tailored for obedience to the Word of God. We're uniquely tailored to deal with challenges. We're uniquely tailored to bring about healing. We're uniquely tailored to bring about peace, to bring about change. We're uniquely tailored to be a family, uniquely tailored to be woke.

We're no longer about pride, greed, or licentiousness. In other words, we weren't cut away to be the same. We were cut away to be distinct. We were cut away to be something new. "Therefore if anyone is in Christ, *he is* a new creature; the old things passed away; behold, new things have come" (2 Cor. 5:17 NASB).

We're cut away. But we're not supposed to be arrogant in being cut away. How could we dare to be arrogant? We're supposed to be one sheet together, no matter what color we are. We should feel more at home with people in the Christian family than our own ethnicity. In other words, the best part of our family should be those who have the same eternal blood type, not just the same physical blood type. In *One Blood: Parting Words to the Church on Race,* Dr. John Perkins talks about his twenty-plus-year friendship with Wayne Gordon: "We decided a long time ago that we were going to link arms together—one black brother and one white brother—and we would see where God would take us. . . . When I think about what made our love grow more and more, it was that whenever we were together we were competing to love the other more."[1]

This is important. It grieves my heart to see that we so often treat each other like we're from different bloodlines. We have the same eternal genetic code, yet too often we act like Hatfields and McCoys, the families that carried out a famous feud. God is calling us to be uniquely distinct. Actually, He has already given us what we need. We're fighting from it, not for it. So God has already given us the holiness. We don't try to be holy. We're already holy. We just have to live and reflect that reality in how we respond to one another and the world.

LIVING HOLY

The world should see us as a city, together on a hill. And they should be taking their cues from us. Our holiness is to be demonstrated in how we love God, the people of God, and the non-believer.

It's interesting that the Lord didn't tell His people to "love your own people." The command was to love God's people and the non-believer. "When you reap the harvest of your land, you are not to reap to the very edge of your field or gather the gleanings of your harvest. Do not strip your vineyard bare or gather its fallen grapes. Leave them for the poor and the resident alien; I am the LORD your God" (Lev. 19:9–10). These were an agricultural people. And as they were harvesting their produce, they were supposed to leave the edges of it untouched; when stuff fell off—and whatever was on the edge—it was for the poor and for people who were different. It was an opportunity to display God's love to those who didn't know Him.

Let's bring this closer to home . . .

So I'm sitting on my patio with the flat screen TV and the fire pit going. I'm grilling hotdogs. I'm smoking a brisket and a pork butt. Ministry is happening in my backyard. I'm chilling. And a dude walks past, and I say, "How you doing? Where you from, man?" He says, "I'm from ___." "Oh, you from ___? Cool. Where you staying?" "I'm staying at the inn, but none of the food spots are open. You know any food spots?" I say, "You good man, go ahead and get all you want from the edge of the grill right there to where you are." He's like, "Get all I want?" "Yeah, get all you want." So he starts grabbing hotdogs and brisket and doing his thing.

Then I come outside and start harvesting some herbs for the brisket. And another dude says, "Let me holler at you. What's up with all this letting people just get what they want—there's a lot of land right here. You just gonna let people just grab it?" I say, "Yeah." He says, "How do you do that?" I say, "You see, the reason is because a God named Yahweh told us to leave this wide open for people who pass by just in case they have need." "Your God told you to do that?" "Sure did." "Man, talk to me about Him." "I'm so glad you asked!" And then, you start letting that thing out in the glorious

name of Jesus Christ, and let him know that God wants
him to be a part of the family too—all because you
opened up your overflow for somebody else.

The prayer that Jabez prayed asking for his territory to be extended was not merely for himself. If his territory was extended
that would mean that his missional possibilities extended as well.
That means that if God blesses me by extending my sphere of
influence, I am to be a witness for Jesus Christ in all those places
and especially in my culture.

DO NOT OPPRESS OTHERS

The Lord then begins to impress His people with the requirement
that they not oppress others. "Do not oppress your neighbor or
rob him. The wages due a hired worker must not remain with
you until morning. . . . Do not act unjustly when deciding a case.
Do not be partial to the poor or give preference to the rich; judge
your neighbor fairly" (Lev. 19:13, 15).

When we look at this idea of oppression, it's important as
believers to recognize the beauty of what God wants us to understand: to oppress means to exploit. It means to treat members of
society at a disadvantage, in unjust ways. It means people who
have a privileged position—in order to keep their privilege—utilize structures, mechanisms, and systems as a way to make sure
that those who are poor and who have challenges are not able to
experience the fullness of what God has made available to everyone. That's what oppression is. Oppression is stopping others
from being able to maximize and experience everything that God
has made available to them.

And when we consider this, it's not just that we don't let them
into our stuff. It's that we create ways to ensure it never happens.

We're all familiar with the account in Scripture of King Ahab. He was married to wicked Jezebel, but he was also wicked through and through. He was a man of privilege, yet he chose to oppress a simple man, Naboth, who owned a piece of land that he wanted. Jezebel conspired to have Naboth and his sons killed so King Ahab could have the land. God's judgment was sure: "This is what the LORD says: Have you murdered and also taken possession? . . . In the place where the dogs licked up Naboth's blood, the dogs will also lick up your blood!" (1 Kings 21:19).

That's a hard word. But it shows how displeased God is when His people don't act like family and don't represent Him as holy people. Our call today is to live like a true family. We should be so radical in our care for one another, and for people in general, that the world has to stop and take notice.

We're in a hard place today—in this country and in the church. The level of brokenness is devastating. People are waiting, literally, for the church to say something. They've heard that we're a family and we're supposed to be holy, so there's an expectation that we will have a word of help and hope for the situation. But we're asleep on what is happening and are expending our energies arguing about things instead of empathizing with one another. This is a huge missed opportunity for the church.

Say something happens where I disagree with my wife, and I think I'm right. If I hold my ground, but look up and see that she's crying, what kind of a husband would I be to say, "Babe, you need to just stop crying! Woman up! Wash your face, put on your makeup, and let's go!" I would be a jerk if I did that. You know what my wife needs me to do? She doesn't need me to provide solutions or to fix it. I'm supposed to say, "Really, honey? What happened? I'm so sorry! I don't want you to hurt like this."

What am I saying? We can have empathy for one another even if we disagree, because love comes before agreement. And sometimes we may need to agree, but we just don't know yet until we listen. We need to listen to each other. When I think about how this could look in our country as Christians, my dream is that we would lock arms together as true brothers and sisters. I don't care what your context is. We need to look at one another and say, "You're family." Those two simple words have the potential to change how we relate to one another.

When we see someone who might be our family member being mistreated or victimized, that should elicit a different response than if we had no connection at all. We would marshal all of our resources if our brother, sister, mother, or father was arrested unfairly and incarcerated. We would get on the phone and make calls to find out what needed to happen to make the situation right. We would care because we are family.

We don't have to look alike. There's beauty in the variations of our skin color. But we can rejoice that on the inside we're all trying to look like the same person. We're all trying to look like our elder brother, Jesus, because we're family, and we're holy.

The movie *Soul Food* closed with a powerful scene. Every Sunday the family has a soul food meal at Big Mamma's house. She is the matriarch of the family who keeps everybody together. But when she dies, it all falls apart. No one wants to work hard to keep the family together, so they decide they don't want to have that meal together anymore. Adultery, family loss, job loss, elitism—all of that stuff splits the family up. But something happens when the kitchen catches on fire. Everybody rushes to the house to see what is going on. A young boy stands up and shouts, "Why can't we all be family? We're supposed to be *family*!" And then he starts crying. His tears reach their hearts. And his message connects. Once again they are able to sit down at the table together. Adulterers sit across from adulterers. Highfalutin folks sit across the table from working class folks. And Big Mamma's image appears, and she looks at everybody at the table and smiles. Because the thing she tried to do more than anything else was keep the family together.

That's my prayer for the church. And it was Christ's prayer for the church, that "all of them may be one" (John 17:21 NIV).

I dream of the day when we will wake up and realize that we really are family, and we have the best soul food table on the planet. We are believers in Jesus Christ, and we have all eaten and drunk from Him. Now we need to sit at the table together and remember that we are family. We need to recognize that around that common table are believers from every nation and tribe—black, white, brown, red, yellow. All family. Let's begin by talking about our family history.

PART TWO

BE WILLING TO
ACKNOWLEDGE

IS THE CHURCH ASLEEP?

I was raised during the post–Civil Rights, black power, and black bourgeoisie eras. My father and mother were almost fifty years old when I was born. Since they were born in the early 1920s, former slaves and the children of former slaves did much of their rearing. With this backdrop, I have quite a different upbringing than my peers. Most of my peers' parents were at least one generation behind my parents. It was a bit unnerving for me because my parents were so old school and my friends' parents were much freer in their parenting styles.

So much of my early life was impacted by my parents' rural post-slavery upbringing and their life experiences in the South with whites. They lived a hard life in the south. My dad in particular told stories about racism that were heartbreaking for him and affected him until his recent death in his nineties. One such story is about something that happened when he was less than eleven years old (around the age of my middle son, Nehemiah). My father had to work to help provide for his impoverished family. One of the first of his many jobs was as a worker in a dry cleaner where he learned tailoring and dry-cleaning during this time. On one occasion, eight suits came up missing. The owners of the business blamed my dad.

That night, the police came to my grandfather's home and snatched my father out of bed. They told my grandmother that if she got in the way they would kill her. Her pleas went unanswered as they whisked him away and put him in jail. They beat him to force a confession, but to no avail. My grandmother ran to the home of her white boss. He went to the police station with her, and she almost collapsed when she saw the condition my father was in. He was so brutally beaten that she had trouble recognizing him.

Her boss asked the sheriff what was going on. They explained that they believed my father had stolen eight suits. The gentleman took one look at my father, noticing his age and size, and asked, "How can someone this boy's weight and size carry eight suits?" The policemen stood dumbfounded. The boss then exclaimed, "What would he do with them?" After hearing the reasoning of my mother's boss, they let him go with no apology or explanation. Some of these men were likely seen as upstanding men in the community, keepers of the law, even leaders in their churches.

Later in life, when he was around sixteen years old, my father lied about his age to enter the draft for World War II. At the recruitment office, they learned that he was not eighteen years old yet. When the recruiter rejected his application to go into the army, my dad cried. The recruiter asked, "What's the matter, boy?" My father responded, "I want to go to war! I want out of South Carolina!" Baffled, the recruiter granted his request by lying about my father's age. My father always told us, "Going to two world wars was better than being a black man in the Jim Crow South!"

These and other experiences colored how I was raised to deal with whites, whether Christian or not. Just as my father's experiences impacted my perceptions about race, so my perceptions will mark those of my three sons. Every week, yet another incident involving racial tension splashes across the headlines and dominates our news feeds. I fear for my sons' lives. I have to hold back tears when I deliver "the talk" that every black parent has with their children. The talk is our way of preparing our children for what it means to live in America today.

This is how it works. One generation's pain and fears are passed on to the next . . . and the next and the next. There is a thread that links all of us inexorably to the past. It doesn't mean that we must repeat the sins of racism and bigotry of the past, but it does mean that they impact us in some way.

Family history matters. One of my great privileges as a pastor is to counsel members of my church who are dealing with varying levels of crisis. When persons are working through issues—whether related to marriage, singleness, or raising children—one of the key things to work through is family history. Family history provides a framework for how a person was nurtured in this sinful world. I need to know what circumstances contributed to the person sitting in front of me. Going through family history reveals the components that helped cause the brokenness that the person needs help repairing.

We understand that family history has a deep impact on the life of a person. But it blows my mind that in American Christianity today, we behave as though our familial past has nothing to do with our present. And it's disturbing how dismissive my evangelical brethren can be toward the past and its impact on where we are today with respect to race in this country and in the church. It grieves me that there is such an unwillingness to go there. Nehemiah 1:6 helps us to understand the impact of sin from one generation to the next: "Let your eyes be open and your ears be attentive to hear your servant's prayer that I now pray to you day and night for your servants, the Israelites. I confess the sins we have committed against you. Both I and my father's family have sinned." We can no longer afford to remain asleep to what has happened and what continues to happen. The Woke Church must understand its history.

THE CHURCH AND SLAVERY

In the formation and creation of America, people from Africa were kidnapped and marched from the interior of Africa to be shipped in inhumane conditions across the Atlantic. They were sold to build an economy based on free labor. But it wasn't really free because it cost them their humanity. To justify the treatment of slaves, society marked Africans as less than human. This helped to soothe the conscience of scores of slave owners in the "New World." Racism and genocide in this New World were justified by greed that was and is rooted in the idolatry of self-importance.

> The transatlantic slave trade was responsible for the forced migration of between 12–15 million people from Africa to the Western Hemisphere from the middle of the 15th century to the end of the 19th century. The trafficking of Africans by the major European countries during this period is sometimes referred to by African scholars as the Maafa ('great disaster' in Swahili). It's now considered a crime against humanity.
>
> The slave trade not only led to the violent transportation overseas of millions of Africans but also to the deaths of many millions more. Nobody knows the total number of people who died during slave raiding and wars in Africa, during transportation and imprisonment, or in horrendous conditions during the so-called Middle Passage, the voyage from Africa to the Americas.[1]

It would be wonderful if we could assume that this was simply a cultural issue, that Christians were not involved in this system of slavery. But that is not the case. George Whitefield, Jonathan Edwards, and many others who are considered leaders of our faith were owners of slaves. George Whitefield spoke strongly against slavery in 1740 in an angry, open letter to three southern colonies, "Your dogs are caressed and fondled at your tables; but your slaves who are frequently styled dogs or beasts, have not an equal privilege. They are scarce permitted to pick up the crumbs which fall from their masters' tables. . . . Although I pray God the slaves may never be permitted to get the upper hand, yet should such a thing be permitted by Providence, all good men must acknowledge the judgment would be just."

Clearly Whitefield understood the evils of slavery. But before we praise him as a great abolitionist, consider this: "by the late 1740s, Whitefield advocated legalizing slavery in Georgia. His concern for orphans had won out over his concern for blacks. . . . Whitefield was not out of step with the times. By 1776, only one denomination in America—the Quakers—had declared slaveholding a sin."[2]

Jonathan Edwards is known to have owned six slaves. In his article "Jonathan Edwards, Slavery, and the Theology of African Americans," Thabiti Anyabwile writes, "We're not surprised, then, that most of our theological heroes from this period—without respect to their theology—remained silent on, justified, and even participated in African enslavement."[3]

The Quakers were a bright light during this period of history. Their activity on behalf of the abolition movement and the Underground Railroad was responsible for the freedom of many slaves. Levi Coffin started helping runaway slaves as a child in North Carolina. Later in his life, Coffin moved to the Ohio-Indiana area, where he became known as the president of the Underground

Railroad. These activities put these people at considerable risk, but they persisted in their work to save many lives.

Slave masters were afraid of blacks gaining literacy or access to the Bible. There was high resistance to slave conversions in approximately the first one-hundred-plus years of slavery. Why? I believe it was because white masters understood the implications of the gospel for the dignity of blacks. If they were introduced to the theology of the *imago dei*, slaves would have understood that they were fully equal with their masters in value. Reading Philemon and 1 Peter 2 would have broken the masters' ungodly hold. As Craig Keener and Glenn Usry write:

> The first American slaveholders did not want their slaves to hear about the Bible, because they feared that the slaves would understand that Christianity made them their masters' equals before God.[4]

Moreover, Albert Raboteau states:

> Slaveholders feared that Christianity would make their slaves not only proud but ungovernable, and even rebellious.[5]

Some historians say there isn't much evidence of slaves being proselytized as a strong movement prior to the Nat Turner revolt. "Nathanial 'Nat' Turner (1800–1831) was a black American slave who led the only effective, sustained slave rebellion (August 1831) in U.S. history. Spreading terror throughout the white South, his action set off a new wave of oppressive legislation prohibiting the education, movement, and assembly of slaves and stiffened pro-slavery, antiabolitionist convictions that persisted in that region until the American Civil War (1861–65)."[6] He believed that God was revealing to him to revolt against the America slave system.

The Nat Turner revolt confirmed some of the suspicions and fears of slave owners. Therefore, they began proselytizing slaves, but placed limits on the nature of the redeeming power of the gospel for them. With the help of clergy, slave owners essentially placed an asterisk on slave discipleship. Moreover, it was an edited version of the true faith intended to keep the slave in a "lesser than" position. The American historian Eugene Genovese explains:

> A great burst of proselytizing among slaves followed the Nat Turner revolt. Whereas previously many slaveholders had feared slaves with religion—and the example of Turner himself confirmed their fears—now they feared slaves without religion even more. They came to see Christianity primarily as a means of social control. Hence the apparent contradictions of the period: a decline of antislavery sentiment in the southern churches; laws against black preachers; laws against teaching slaves to read and write; encouragement of oral instruction of slaves in the Christian faith; and campaigns to encourage more humane treatment of slaves.[7]

In light of this, the American church viewed slavery as a step up from the conditions of the slave in Africa and a help in the process of civilizing the African in America. Churches were only willing to encourage the conversion of blacks if their understanding of the gospel and the Scriptures was limited. However, this strategy would not last long. The gospel rebels against anything that attempts to stifle its power. Ultimately, the liberty that is inherent in the nature of the gospel is impossible to obscure. Yet, many whites attempted to do just that.

With a few notable exceptions, each denomination made its own accommodation in due time, and the schism of the northern and southern branches merely strengthened a *fait accompli*. Thus, the General Assembly of the Presbyterian Church declared in 1861 that the slave system had generally proven "kindly and benevolent" and had provided "real effective discipline" to a people who could not be elevated in any other way. Slavery, it concluded, was the black man's "normal condition."[8]

Many modern mainline denominations played a role in soothing the conscience of those involved in the oppression of slavery by creating theologies and ideologies that justified these atrocities. One such ideology was that blackness was a curse. This was used to communicate black inferiority. Poor biblical theology created the so-called "Curse of Ham," a bizarre misappropriation of the curse Noah pronounced on his grandson Canaan, not his son Ham, which was said to apply to all black people of Africa and beyond. Several works have documented that Christianity adapted this from the ancient Black Moors and Arabian Muslims. There are key differences in how its implications worked out, but this is the proposed origin of the fallacy.

> Historians Bernard Lewis and William McKee Evans have presented much evidence to support the view that the Islamic world preceded the Christian in representing sub-Saharan Africans as descendants of Ham, who were cursed and condemned to perpetual bondage because of their ancestor's mistreatment of his father, Noah, as described in an obscure passage in Genesis.[9]

Although this quote reflects its influence on the slave trade, this heretical fable found its way into the anthropology of American Christianity and can be felt up to the present day. The idea that blacks were cursed helped cement the creation of a black and a white church as two separate entities in the United States. Black churches started before the end of slavery, but exploded after Reconstruction because of continued racial bias by white Christian churches.

THE CHURCH POST-SLAVERY

From Black Codes to Jim Crow, the church's witness during this time in history is troubling. The Ku Klux Klan started in Pulaski, Tennessee, in 1866 to resist the Republican Party's efforts during Reconstruction to establish the economic and political equality of blacks. The KKK did "off the record" work to terrorize blacks and any whites who were sympathetic to blacks in the South. Here's how one observer from the time described the Klan's resurgence and the church's muted response.

> In the south after 1865, the condemnation of racism invited retaliation by secret societies. One such society was the Ku Klux Klan (KKK). During Reconstruction, the Klan terrorized Republicans, persecuted blacks, and intimidated scalawags. The 1920s witnessed a rebirth of the KKK in the United States. Again the Protestant churches responded in a variety of ways. While most denominations deplored the covert activities of the Klan, few spoke out directly and publicly condemned the Klan: "The attitude of the Protestant churches towards the Klan as reflected in the minutes of national conventions assemblies and councils reveals resolutions

deploring lynching and mob violence, but none referred to the Ku Klux Klan."[10]

Vigilante squads had their first mass meeting at the First Baptist Church according to *The Hidden History of Tulsa* by Steve Gerkin. In "1915, the second incarnation of the Ku Klux Klan was born. . . . The second Klan required its members to be not only white and male but also Christian. Religion became the centerpiece of the second Klan's platform, and Klansmen showed their allegiance to their faith through church attendance, speeches and writings and the recruitment of ministers as members."[11]

The story of Black Wall Street provides a disturbing illustration of the unholy alliance between the church and the KKK. Black Wall Street was in the Greenwood section of Tulsa, Oklahoma, where affluent blacks lived and flourished among thriving black businesses and a sense of cultural renaissance.

> Detroit Avenue, along the edge of Standpipe Hill, contained a number of expensive houses belonging to doctors, lawyers and business owners. The buildings on Greenwood Avenue housed the offices of almost all of Tulsa's black lawyers, realtors, doctors, and other professionals. Deep Greenwood, as the area at the intersection of Greenwood and Archer Avenues was known, served as a model African-American community to towns worldwide. Greenwood was a very religiously active community. At the time of the racial violence there were more than two dozen black American churches and many Christian youth organizations and religious societies.[12]

The citizens of Tulsa didn't like the flourishing of blacks in Greenwood, so they created a diversion to cover one of the greatest state-supported massacres in US history.

> That wealth infuriated White residents and business owners, and their anger exploded on May 31, 1921. According to The Tulsa Historic Society and Museum, police arrested a Black man named Dick Rowland on suspicion that he assaulted Sarah Page, a White woman, in an elevator the previous day. Local newspapers circulated unsubstantiated reports about Rowland allegedly raping Page, and an armed White group confronted a similarly armed Black group of World War I veterans outside the courthouse where the sheriff held Rowland. The two sides exchanged shots until the outnumbered Black militia, initially trying to prevent a lynching, had to retreat.
>
> White Tulsans then attacked the Greenwood neighborhood for two days. Smithsonian Magazine says the mobs destroyed 35 blocks and killed almost 300 Black people. Police and the National Guard intervened primarily to put out building fires and arrest Black people, some of whom were taken out of vigilante custody. Franklin says that White rioters, aided by city government and the National Guard, "were deputized and handed weapons" to carry out the massacre.
>
> But while anger towards Rowland may have lit the fuse, Franklin says the riots systematically targeted Black wealth.[13]

Although almost all the black churches in Greenwood were destroyed by the angry mob, they skipped the First Baptist Church. "Notably, First Baptist Church of North Tulsa was spared— spared because it was mistaken for a white church."[14] The incident was categorized as a race riot, because this designation would allow the insurance companies to refuse reimbursement to the Greenwood residents for their loss of property.

Where was the church's prophetic voice in response to this massacre? Well, a few white churches collected clothes, bedding, and other goods for a few days in response to an ad requesting help in rebuilding Greenwood after the fire. But the response from a particular white pastor threw cold water on those efforts and a different perspective prevailed. The pastor of Centenary Methodist Church claimed that the black population was solely responsible for the riot. Not surprisingly, Centenary became known as the primary gathering place of the Tulsa chapter of the KKK during this time in Tulsa's history.

You might think that this was an isolated incident, but nothing could be further from the truth. Cities across the country experienced similar events: Atlanta race riots of 1906, Chicago race riots of 1919, the Rosewood massacre of 1923, Washington, D.C. riots of 1919, Knoxville, Tennessee, race riots of 1919, and the East Saint Louis race riots of 1917. All of these efforts were moved to both systemically destroy the opportunity for blacks to build wealth and served as the foundation of building a mythological legacy of "black laziness."

In 1930, Dietrich Bonhoeffer learned from the black church (Abyssinian Baptist Church in Harlem, New York) how his experience under the Christian-endorsed Nazi regime paralleled the experience of racism and injustice in the United States. His encounter with the black church "allowed him to empathize with the suffering of marginalized people so deeply that, on his return to Germany, the devilish spirit of Hitler's National Socialism was readily apparent."[15] He wondered how America's theology could allow us to perpetuate injustice and racism against the American negro. He railed against the false dichotomies in our theology, particularly our view of comprehensive gospel transformation. He writes:

God has granted American Christianity no Reformation. He has given it strong revivalist preachers, churchmen and theologians, but no Reformation of the church of Jesus Christ by the Word of God. . . . American theology and the American church as a whole have never been able to understand the meaning of "criticism" by the Word of God and all that signifies. Right to the last they do not understand that God's "criticism" touches even religion, the Christianity of the church and the sanctification of Christians, and that God has founded his church beyond religion and beyond ethics. . . . In American theology, Christianity is still essentially religion and ethics. . . . Because of this, the person and work of Christ must, for theology, sink into the background and in the long run remain misunderstood, because it is not recognized as the sole ground of radical judgment and radical forgiveness.[16]

THE CHURCH IN CIVIL RIGHTS

When we talk about civil rights in America, we have to talk about Dr. Martin Luther King Jr. It is impossible to look at his ministry and his writings and not see the gospel in it. His *Letter from a Birmingham Jail* reveals the overall sentiment of the evangelical church during that time. His words are just as true and prophetic now as they were then:

I have heard numerous southern religious leaders admonish their worshipers to comply with a desegregation decision because it is the law, but I have longed to hear white ministers declare: "Follow this decree because integration is morally right and because the Negro is your brother." In the midst of blatant injustices inflicted upon the Negro, I have watched white churchmen stand on the sideline and mouth pious irrelevancies and sanctimonious trivialities. In the midst of a mighty struggle to rid our nation of racial and economic injustice, I have heard many ministers say: "Those are social issues, with which the gospel has no real concern." And I have watched many churches commit themselves to a completely other worldly religion which makes a strange, un-Biblical distinction between body and soul, between the sacred and the secular.[17]

His indictment here is quite enough. Although he had allies, evangelicalism's theology wasn't robust enough to include his mission. Evangelicalism and reformed circles have always prided themselves for being "theologically robust." If our theology isn't wide enough to fit racial equality and fighting injustice within it, then, my friend, our theology is wanting.

One of the events that galvanized the early Civil Rights movement was the abduction and murder of fourteen-year-old Emmitt Till. Emmett was born in 1941 in Chicago and grew up in a middle-class black neighborhood. He was visiting relatives in Money, Mississippi, in 1955 when he was accused of whistling at Carolyn Bryant, a white woman who was a cashier at a grocery store. Four days later, her husband and brother kidnapped Emmett, then brutally beat him, shot him, and threw his body in the river. The men were tried for murder, but an all-white, male jury acquitted them. In a 2007 interview, Carolyn admitted that she had lied about Emmett making advances toward her.[18]

The Civil Rights movement of the 1960s, while politically motivated, raised fundamental issues for the black church and for American Christianity as well. Once the Montgomery, Alabama, campaign for civil rights and human dignity had caught the imagination of black people everywhere, the integrity of the black church itself became an issue.

While the movement was galvanizing the hearts of black Christians, evangelical and fundamentalist Christian colleges were struggling with how to deal with racism without upsetting too many folks or appearing to side with the "lawbreakers" of the Civil Rights movement. Faculty and students who saw racism as a systemic problem requiring an institutional response were met at every turn by the insistence that individual conversion was the only answer." Schools like Bob Jones University made the strategic decision to not admit black students as a way to prevent interracial dating and marriage.[19]

I would say that the Civil Rights era created a greater schism than already existed because it highlighted the differences in how the black church and the white church responded to the issue of racism. White evangelicalism's lack of involvement in the movement as a whole hurt our long-term relationships with one another. Even to this day, the black church has never forgotten the brash disconnect of Christian conservativism's silence or verbal support of segregation.

THE CHURCH IN THE MODERN ERA

We are at the cusp of another church movement that will determine the trajectory of the church in America for some time to come. Whether they call it "race battle fatigue" or post-traumatic stress, many black Christians have expressed frustration and weariness of fighting this battle within the church. Many are just done with evangelicalism. The popular rapper Lecrae shared a similar sentiment in his interview about "divorcing white evangelicalism" on Truth Table's podcast.[20] Whatever you think of

Lecrae's decision, his choice reflects a broader sense of frustration among African Americans. We are tired of arguing about race and injustice.

Many African Americans who engage the white church end up feeling like pawns for diversity instead of true agents of gospel change. When they speak out against injustice and white silence, they find themselves sidelined. Their unwillingness to "keep the peace" results in losing a place at the table.

One of the by-products of the refusal of evangelicals as a whole to engage the issue of racism and justice is the rise of Black Nationalism. For many African Americans, the appeal of the Nation of Islam, Hebrew Israelites, and the Black Consciousness Community and other such organizations is increasing day by day. They see their purpose as the restoration of black dignity and respect. These are huge needs in the black community. And the appeal is made much stronger against the specter of a church that is still divided along racial lines.

Growing up in D.C., I can attest to the influence of the Nation of Islam. In the middle of broken black neighborhoods, you would see freshly shaven black men wearing suits and bow ties and promoting black dignity. I looked up to them and wanted to be like them. In many ways, they were effective in helping blacks feel a sense of worth and dignity. They had a handshake and the greeting of peace that spoke of brotherhood, connection, and respect. One of their staples has been their commitment to developing and raising up black men. One of their senior leaders, Malcolm X, was known for his rhetorical genius and his love for his people. He argued that the Bible was being twisted to fit an agenda aimed at the continued enslavement of blacks.

In the early '90s, conscious hip-hop broke out like a fire: Dead Prez, X-Clan, Public Enemy, and Poor Righteous Teachers were among some of the most noted in the genre for their socially and sometimes spiritually aware art. Other groups laced their black power ideology with slick slang that only the streets could discern. Much of their lyrical content was pro-black and anti-Christian. Some of their content made admitting you were a Christian embarrassing. I was a college student at the time and remember being drawn to these ideologies because of their commitment to black dignity. However, I didn't understand that I was yearning for the dignity that God gives all people. I was willing to hear it from anywhere. I sat in black history classes, talked on the quad, read books, and studied non-Christian religions to find it. As I swept through many black mystery cults and ideologies, I could agree with the sociology and some of the practical desires, but something seemed off.

Many African Americans have experienced more affirmation of our dignity from black power movements than we have from the church of Jesus Christ. Pastor Tony Evans expresses this well:

> To refer to myself as a black evangelical means that I am a man who has been doubly influenced. On the one hand I have had the distinct mark of the black experience indelibly etched on my life. That means I, like most black baby boomers, have known the good and bad of being black in America. It means I have experienced the ravages of racism while also having partaken of the great history and culture of African American life.
>
> On the other hand it also means I have been profoundly influenced by white evangelicalism. I have studied in its institutions, interfaced with its . . . leadership on its epistemological and theological worldview. I have integrated some of its perspectives and values into my own life and ministry.
>
> It is unfortunate, though, that my appreciation and

legitimate pride in my race was not provided me by my study of Christian theology. Instead, it came as a result of the civil rights movement. It was not until the social revolution of this era that I, like many of my contemporaries, developed a new awareness, appreciation, and awakened self-consciousness of blackness.[21]

The arguments waged by Black Nationalist organizations are the most common obstacle to evangelism and mission to blacks in the inner city and on college campuses. This puts black evangelical Christians in an uncomfortable dilemma. We struggle to share the faith in a context that charges that our religion is a tool to keep us in our place. At the same time, we occupy a place of feeling "lesser than" within the white evangelical context. It's a hard place to be. Yet our call is to preach the liberating gospel—and believe that this gospel can tear down centuries-old walls that divide.

The truth is that we have not been at this freedom thing for long at all. Consider this chart that pictures the timeline from the system of slavery to segregation and beyond:[22]

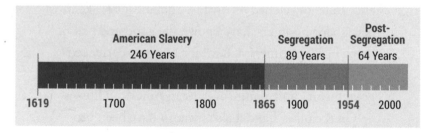

We've made progress from the overt institution of slavery . . . we've moved past separate but equal . . . but we have so much farther to go.

These may be hard truths to hear; but this is my heart. This is the heart and the experience of a people, my people, your people. We are one. We are family. This is our history. The strings of our family history have tethered us to a past that binds the present and tempts us to continue the conspiracy of silence. Or we can wake up from our slumber!

THINGS FOR THE CHURCH TO LAMENT

In Jewish tradition, the first word of a biblical book often serves as the book's title. So the Hebrew title of Lamentations is *eikhah*, which means "Alas" or "O how."[1] In the Greek translation of the Old Testament, it is called "Dirge" or "Dirge of Jeremiah." The simple meaning is expression of grief. It's a frustrating question to God. God, how? Some would say, Alas! Soong Chan Rah points out that the psalms have a metered version that usually has a pitty-pat rhythm—but if I had been one of the writers under the inspiration of the Holy Spirit, I would have named Lamentations Redemptive Blues. I'm not talking about R&B; I'm talking about the blues: it's heavy like that.

Lament is about entering into the experience of brokenness and being honest about it. I admit that I am a novice at lamenting. Frankly, I'm out of my element because lament draws out the emotions that I don't want to deal with. Jews often revisited their awful past in order to never forget what had happened. God gave them freedom to remember the brokenness of what had happened to them. When America tells African Americans to forget about the past when we haven't even talked about it, that's unhealthy. In biblical times, when somebody died in your family, you got a month off work to grieve, and then other people could take time off and come around you to grieve with you—or sit and say nothing. They might just rock back and forth and put their hand on you and not say a word. That's biblical lament.

The people of Israel looked back on the past and never forgot how they got in the predicament they were in. And they learned from it. Not only that, they could see the work of the Lord through it. They could view the brokenness of their past as spiritual formation for the present. If they had not revisited the brokenness of their past, they would have missed out on a key opportunity for spiritual formation.

In Lamentations 3:1, the prophet says, "I am the man who has seen affliction under the rod of God's wrath." He says, "I am the man who has seen affliction." He's saying, "I'm an eyewitness to the brokenness that has happened to my people." He's going to talk about how bitter he is. He's going to talk about how God has knocked his teeth out. He's seen a lot of suffering. When you actually see the suffering, you must lament.

And what have we seen in our cities? Many of us have made the choice to get as far from the inner city as possible—to remove ourselves from the pain and suffering. When I was in Dallas and had my first experience really living outside the inner city, I said I'd never go into the inner city again. But God has a sense of humor. I said, "I'm not going." He said, "You're going." When you grow up in the inner city, you never want to go back. You're thinking, "I'm about to get this degree, I'm about to get some mock necks, some shoes, some outfits, and a loft downtown. I'm gonna be in a loft looking out over the city, looking like Tony Montana, but legal."

I had a plan. But God had a different plan for me. I wanted

to look down from the loft. God wanted me back on the block. I found myself in the inner city of Dallas working with Bloods, Crips, Gangstas, and East Dallas Locos. I was sharing the gospel beside housing projects and hearing the stories of young girls and young boys who were exposed to things that children should never be exposed to. I remember those days.

I remember seeing zombie-looking parents—their minds gone from PCP—who didn't even know who they were, but still had a baby in diapers that hadn't been changed in two days. I remember the rampant prostitution. I remember how some black men had to hide the fact that they were living with their children's mothers. In order for the mother to get on welfare, she had to be single. But in order to get more money she had to have more children.

We've seen suffering. And we need to lament what has happened in this country—the division in our culture and in the church. I lament raising Immanuel, Nehemiah, and Ephraim in a country that makes me fearful that they will become a hashtag one day. I didn't name them to be a hashtag. My first son's name means *God with us*. The second one means *Yahweh comforts*. The third one means *God has made me fruitful in the land of my affliction*.

When I named them, I didn't want them to be a hashtag for being murdered. So I lament that as I'm telling my son in his teenage years to listen to the police, I'm fearful that he will become a statistic. I worry they all could become statistics. Why is all of this important? Because we have to have room in the church to be honest with where we are. We have to learn not to fix people real quick when they begin sharing their hearts and their hurts. If God can listen, so can we.

When the realities of a fallen world hit us, we need room to worship the Lord in honest expressions of unedited grief. This chapter is about this very thing. Entering the pain of others and pains we should all feel and bear together. This isn't a chapter about solutions, but coming to terms with the fact that we have deep problems. So what are some of the realities that we need to lament?

Lament #1: The Fact that the Black Church Had to Be Created

The founding of the first black denomination came from a refusal to accept black people in the church as equal in every respect. Richard Allen and Absalom Jones, former slaves, were attendees at the St. George's Episcopal Church in Philadelphia, Pennsylvania, in 1787. Blacks and whites were allowed to worship together, as long as they were in separate spaces. We have the words of Richard Allen to explain the event that led to the formation of the first black denomination:

> A number of us usually attended St. George's Church on Fourth Street; and when the coloured people began to get numerous in attending the church, they moved us from the seats we usually sat on, and placed us around the wall, and on Sabbath morning we went to church and the sexton stood at the door, and told us to go in the gallery. He told us to go, and we would see where to sit. We expected to take the seats over the ones we formerly occupied below, not knowing any better. We took those seats. Meeting had begun, and they were nearly done singing, and just as we got to the seats, the elder said, "Let us pray." We had not been long upon our knees before I heard considerable scuffling and low talking. I raised my head up and saw one of the trustees, H— M—, having hold Rev. Absalom Jones, pulling him up off of his knees, and saying, "You must get up—you must not kneel here." Mr. Jones replied, "Wait until prayer is over."

Mr. H— M— said "no, you must get up now, or I will call for aid and force you away." Mr. Jones said, "wait until prayer is over, and I will get up and trouble you no more." With that he beckoned to one of the other trustees, Mr. L— S— to come to his assistance. He came, and went to William White to pull him up. By this time prayer was over, and we all went out of the church in a body, and they were no more plagued with us in the church.[2]

Rev. Richard Allen and Rev. Absalom Jones left and formed the African Methodist Episcopal Church. Blacks didn't seek this as a primary goal. The separation flowed from the white church's unwillingness to preach and live out a full gospel. How astounding is it that the black church exists, not as an entity that was born out of willing missiological effort, but out of heretical theology and practice.

Lament #2: Evangelicals' Dismissal of the Black Church

I often hear from evangelicals that "there is no such thing as the black church." I grieve this statement because it reflects a disregard for the uniqueness and the value of this institution. I lament that there was a need for a separate church for blacks, but I value and affirm how God has used the black church to accomplish His purposes.

I am a product of the black church. The black church is where I found identity, significance, and purpose—from Vacation Bible School, substance abuse prevention, singing in choirs, trips to conferences, surrogate parents, discipline, and encouragement. That is the first place I was told I could sing, the first place I was told my voice mattered, the first place to hear someone say, "God's hand is on you for a mighty work."

Yet today, its existence is being questioned. I fear that with all of the multiethnic congregations being formed, we will lose the focus on engaging the systemic needs of blacks. Many times in multiethnic spaces, others get primacy and the needs of blacks are minimized. It almost feels like in order for the church to be one, blacks have to merge with whites as the standard church, then we spend the rest of our lives trying to "integrate" a system that wants us present, but is not willing to shape the central systems to make room for all people.

I grieve that we might never experience a viable unity that is equitable to all and empathetic to the black experience in America. I fear that if we partner with whites that they will find a way to subjugate blacks and make us dependent on them in a way that kills our freedom of a truly black led institution. We need places where we don't have to nuance and explain every little thing.

Barbara Skinner helps to articulate this in an article she wrote in the 1996 edition of *Reconciler* magazine called "Been There, Done That." She explains, "While there is no excuse for allowing racial barriers to stand, many African American Christians have trouble getting excited about reconciliation." Blacks fear losing the last truly African-American institution—their churches. This quote explains one of the reasons why:

> The black Church is one of the few institutions totally owned and controlled by African Americans. An estimated 65,000 churches—reaching 16 million people each week—are some of the few places African Americans can witness strong and dynamic black leadership at all levels, build social and leadership skills, advance their political and public policy interests, improve their communities, and reach inner-city youth and those needing financial help to attend college. At the same

time, like nowhere else, they receive spiritual encouragement for the struggles of life. Indeed, the Church is our last and most important refuge of empowerment.

In the age of serious moral crisis of black family break-down, drugs, and crime, "reconciliation" seems like a strange diversion of precious energy and resources to a cause with little chance of success. Surely reconciliation is a higher calling than separation—but not if the definition of reconciliation sacrifices the empowerment of African Americans. In the name of integration, Blacks lost many of the institutions that addressed their needs: businesses, self-help organizations, and schools. Can they trust the new form of "reconciliation" to address their needs and give room for black leadership? Past experience answers a resounding "No."[3]

I'm not sure there is a quick solution to this complex problem. My desire isn't to find a quick fix. I grieve the complexities of removing the racial barriers without having to give up on the need for a focused gospel ministry to the pressing needs of blacks in this country.

Lament #3: Tokenism

Some friends sent me a link to a major white ministry's website that was doing a conference. Most of the speakers on the main stage were white men. They pointed me to a segment of the conference that was focused on urban ministry. All of the speakers were black men. They were grieved because few of the black men were experts in the field of urban ministry. Most of them were either just landing as leaders in urban ministry or had been in it a short time. Many of us couldn't help but wonder, *would they select whites who were novices to train others on major issues?*

Tokenism is damaging to reconciliation. When blacks who lack significant expertise are given this kind of platform, it suggests that there is not authentic care for the subject matter. My grief in this area is strong because this continues to happen again and again. It represents a frail attempt to have blacks present but not a part of the big stage conversation. My friend Bryan Loritts sees this as well, and we lament together.

> I'm tired of recommending young minority leaders to serve on white church staffs, and watching them get used as tokens to show how "serious" the church is about diversity, only to see it end very badly.
>
> I'm tired of the silence of other minority leaders who, in their pursuit of climbing Mount Significance, are scared to speak the truth for fear of not being invited to some conference, missing out on a book deal, and not having their brand established or extended.[4]

Tokenism impacts whites as well. If an unqualified black man or woman is brought into a majority white space as a professional integrationist or just as a black presence to promote diversity, but lacks the acumen for the role, it hurts. It hurts whites who may not have experienced blacks in these spaces because it could mark their interaction as standard or the norm. I understand the importance of making attempts at diversity, but many times they can be a train wreck if not well planned and strategically thought through. I can't tell you how many conversations I've had with white leaders frustrated with young blacks who they didn't realize were not qualified as leaders. If whites hire African Americans that African Americans don't follow or respect, these persons will not be helpful in attracting other blacks. This issue could be solved by simply connecting with the spiritual leaders from their past. Bypassing biblical and cultural protocol can do damage to the ministry on all fronts.

Lament #4: Racial Insensitivity in the Academy

I have a master's degree and a doctorate from two amazing seminaries. One is located in the south and the second in the far northeast, in the shadow of Ivy League schools and liberal intellectualism. I'm grateful for the perspectives each have played in my theological education. All educational institutions have their own perspectives and biases. That's true of theological institutions as well. Doing theology will include processing it through one's cultural grid. All theology is done that way. I think that in most evangelical academic spheres, there can be blindness regarding what is cultural and what is biblical. Our understanding of community is processed culturally, our soteriology is processed culturally, and our understanding of spiritual growth is as well. Our cultural perspective comes through clearly in how we depict church history.

Much of Christian history is painted white. It is almost the norm for Turkish, Mediterranean, African, and biblical characters to be assumed to be white. But many of the most notable church fathers were of North African descent: Augustine, Clement, Origen, Tertullian, Athanasius, and Cyril. My cry here isn't for diversity, but honest portrayals of history. We need healthy research that communicates fidelity to God, others, and history.

If we aren't clear on a historical figure's exact ethnic identity, the default color shouldn't be white. When we talk about North African, we assume Roman or Latin, not African or indigenous to the continent. German Lutheran theologian and church historian Adolph von Harnack and others helped to perpetuate this false thinking.

The generalization took hold that wherever there might have been any modest African influences, they are likely to be viewed as inferior and backward in relation to the unfolding positive developments of reason in history that flowed from Europe. The companion premise is that if good ideas appeared in Africa, they must be attributed to Europeans. This bizarre habit consistently viewed the Alexandrian and Egyptian Christians as entirely disconnected from African ways. To deprive Africa of Alexandria is to say that a blossom is unrelated to its climate.[5]

The mistrust many blacks experience in evangelism and gospel mission flows from this. I grieve as I talk to Hebrew Israelites, people in African Kemetic and Yoruba religions, black atheists, and agnostics. They all point to the ways that they see Christian scholarship as married to the history of prejudice that seeks to destroy black dignity. When I tell them that the gospel is able to restore our dignity, I'm viewed as one who is asleep instead of one who is truly woke. I'm heartbroken as I watch many of my black brothers and sisters take in the demonic poison that flows from the unintended consequences of scholarly prejudice and willful negligence.

Lament #5: Evangelical Perception of Black Preachers

I remember being on a panel about race. A well-meaning white brother mentioned how encouraged he was to see so many young black leaders in the room who are being raised up to preach a "robust gospel" *finally*. Three of us at the event didn't see that as a compliment. We saw it as an extremely uninformed perspective on black preaching. I grieve this narrative. Contrary to popular belief, all black preachers do not preach the prosperity gospel or see social justice as the content of the gospel. Most black preachers I know have—as a part of their training—the centrality of Jesus, the gospel, and the cross. To be honest, that is where I learned to preach the cross and center on Jesus. When I was in seminary, a black Baptist brother named Hilliard from Bunkie, Louisiana, used to exhort all of us to keep Jesus in our preaching.

At another conference on Christ-centered preaching, there was a strong argument that a sect of white evangelicalism known as the neo-reformed movement was recovering Christ-centered preaching. I was confused about this narrative that suggests that white evangelicals are saving the history of Christianity in the West. We study Spurgeon and call him the "prince of preaching". Yet the greatest preacher of our generation, in my estimation, is Gardener C. Taylor. He is known as the dean of black preachers. He is viewed as an American treasure. *Christianity Today* referred to him as the "last pulpit prince."[6] He never lost his focus on Jesus or the cross. He has inspired many of us to keep the cross at the center and Jesus as the hero. He says, "without the incarnation of Jesus, we would have a murky and opaque and unclear picture of what God is like."

The lack of knowledge and familiarity with preaching giants like Gardener Taylor leads many to believe that there is a lack of sound theological preaching in the black church. This limited exposure to black preaching creates reductionist views and untrue caricatures.

Lament #6: That Justice Is Not Seen as a Primary Doctrine

In Matthew 23:23, we notice that Jesus says that justice is one of the weightier matters of the law. Also, we know that the principles of the law pervade the entire biblical narrative. Our Lord expected us to judge all of life rightly or see it rightly based on the Word. Micah named justice as a core desire of Yahweh for

His people. We in the West seem to have what I call Selective Justice Syndrome (SJS). We select comfortable forms of justice to address; even then we don't view it as central to the mission of God. Solomon administered justice between the women fighting over the baby. In other words, he judged. Western Christianity must do so in the area of racial injustice. My grief comes from the battle fatigue of trying to convince people who have some of the greatest theological libraries and access to ancient manuscripts, yet don't see justice as a central Bible doctrine.

In a recent conversation on Twitter, three black Christian leaders and I were accused of dividing the Lord's Table by talking about race and black dignity. We were called to ascribe to "color-blindness." While that might be a comfortable position for some, "color-blindness" denies God's promise to Abraham that "in you all the nations shall be blessed" (Gal. 3:8 NKJV). It denies the Father's promise to the Son that "I will also make you a light for the nations" (Isa. 49:6). It denies the Spirit's promise to us that all the peoples will praise God (see Ps. 67:5). It denies Christ's great commission to disciple the nations. It denies the Spirit's work to prepare us for a multiethnic table. In Acts 10, the Lord prepares Peter with a vision, not only to preach to Gentiles but also to accept them as clean/equals in Christ. Color-blind theology denies one of the main tenets of the historic Christian faith as outlined in the Apostles' Creed: "I believe in the holy catholic Church." Catholicity means precisely the opposite of colorblindness—celebrating the inclusion of all ethnicities in Christ. Colorblind theology denies Christ's power to heal racial divisions, disparities, and injustices by ignoring their ongoing impact. Colorblind theology undermines unity in the church by refusing to acknowledge significant ethnic differences or address significant problems.

I would say that Micah has a robust theology of justice being a weighty matter of Scripture as well as a central Bible doctrine. His theological eye was able to scope the Scriptures and apply justice hermeneutics—not in competition with the gospel of regeneration but as an outworking of it. We grieve because white Christian leaders who are able to see hendiadys, dangling participles, Nifil stems in Hebrew, and Aorist passives, and can excavate archeological finds of Hittite culture and frame the unknown alphabet are unable to see racism and injustice. This is lament-worthy.

Lament #7: That the Church Didn't Create and Lead the Black Lives Matter Movement

In August of 2016, I was at a large event on the Washington National Mall. I spoke to hundreds of thousands of people and met the grandmother of Philando Castile, the man who was killed in front of his daughter and girlfriend. Talking to her gave me a peek behind the scenes of what happens to families after unjust killings like this. When the officer who committed this act was released, many blacks protested, as this event added to a long string of publicized killings. Many evangelicals made some very unfortunate and non-empathetic statements. In light of the early killings, a hashtag turned into an organization called Black Lives Matter.

In the eyes of many, Black Lives Matter has become the voice of black dignity. "Black Lives Matter is an ideological and political intervention in a world where Black lives are systematically and intentionally targeted for demise. It is an affirmation of Black folks' humanity, our contributions to this society, and our resilience in the face of deadly oppression."[7] As #BlackLivesMatter gained momentum throughout 2013 and 2014, "we utilized it as a platform and organizing tool. Other groups, organizations, and individuals used it to amplify anti-Black racism across the country.... Tamir Rice, Tanisha Anderson, Mya Hall, Walter Scott,

Sandra Bland"—these victims are important and must not be forgotten. #BlackLivesMatter "helped propel the conversation around the state-sanctioned violence they experienced."[8]

Why do I lament? The reason I lament this is because the church should have been the leader of this movement. Christians of all ethnicities should have entered their pulpits and gone to war in the fight for black lives, both in these instances and holistically. We should have been quoting Isaiah 10:1–3, "Woe to those enacting crooked statutes and writing oppressive laws to keep the poor from getting a fair trial and to deprive the needy among my people of justice, so that widows can be their spoil and they can plunder the fatherless. What will you do on the day of punishment when devastation comes from far away? Who will you run to for help? Where will you leave your wealth?"

Our voices should have lifted in unison against assaults on black life. Black pastors, white pastors, Asians, Latinos—all should have spoken out. We should have hit the streets together ringing out against these injustices. Instead we argued and minimized these events. Now we are dealing with schism, and our witness to the broader world has suffered in large part because of our silence and inaction.

Lament #8: Diminished Presence on Justice Issues

I participated in a BET documentary for rapper T.I. "Us or Else" as a representative of the church. Angela Rye moderated the discussion, and there was a host of other leaders and activists. It was interesting to see so many people in this generation talking about the issues of racial injustice and inequality. As I listened, it became apparent that they had a high expectation for the black church to engage these matters. They wondered where the black church has been in addressing today's justice issues beyond pulpit rhetoric.

I pastor a church full of Millennials and serve scores of pastors who engage them. The burning question they have: Where is the voice and vocation of the black church as a movement leader? Rye asked, "Where is the black church today?" I know I might be breaking black church etiquette, but I have wondered the same thing. I have grieved as one who is a product of the black church. Even in the '90s when I was in college and dealing with the Nation of Islam, I couldn't find a church that was equipping us to challenge it. For me, this is painful because I don't think this is something we lack the ability to do. I believe this is a focus issue. We don't tend to engage this stuff until it becomes an issue of loss of membership.

In the past, the black church has engaged issues of racial injustice, both theologically and practically. I'm not sure why we seem reluctant to do the same today. Is this lack of focus because of the decentralization of black life in the post–Civil Rights era? Or is it perhaps because of the many immediate needs that seem more pressing? Whatever the reason, we don't seem to be moving toward change. In spite of those realities in the past, we always found a way to fight!

In our own city, we do an analysis every year. We ask our community: What are the top three needs in the community? What are the three greatest influences? And what are the churches in this community doing to put a dent in those three needs? By and large, our community has viewed the churches in the community as absent and more concerned about themselves than they are about the community. We are not talking about meeting every need, but our actions should clearly communicate its love for neighborhoods in all of our cities, particularly broken and hopeless communities.

Lament #9: Not Effectively Equipping the Church to Know How to Engage Black Ideologies

Pastors reach out to me about how to engage black ideologies: Pan Africanism, the Nation of Islam, the Moorish Science Temple, and other groups. There is a growing concern that these cults are drawing Christians away from the church because of their strong appeal to black dignity. Black Christians are seeing memes and watching videos on the Internet that suggest that Christianity lacks validity and is the white man's religion. Much of it is pseudo-scholarship. However, because of the acute need for black dignity in the Americas and Caribbean, these ideologies are meeting a need that has gone largely unmet by the church.

Through our church's initiative, Thriving, we are engaging these ideologies by equipping the church. We have a host of resources: the Urban Perspective, led by Jerome Gay; Jude 3 Project, led by Lisa Fields; Urbanlogia Ministries, led by Damon Richardson; and Urban Apologetics, led by Muhammed Tanzymore and Vince Bantu; and articles by Ernest Grant and a host of other media (Berean TV, Nefer Nitty, Adam Coleman TruID Podcast). But these efforts, as great as they are, are tiny barriers against the tidal wave on the Internet. Many ex-Christians and even ex-pastors use pseudo-scholarship to discredit Christianity. One of the saddest stories in recent days was that of a black pastor in Texas handing the keys of his church over to black Hebrew Israelites. Not all, but most Hebrew Israelites teach that they are the true Israel, that Jesus was black, and heaven and hell are a state of mind—not metaphysical realities. The church of God was converted to a cult.

I am grieved. We are reaping the bitter fruit of a black identity crisis that I know the gospel is sufficient to fill. But we have let this fester for years. There was a small crop of books written in the

'90s that denounced these ideologies, but it is time we enter the ring and defend the gospel in our generation. Black pastors have to lead the charge, and they don't have to have a seminary degree to do so. We must become students of what the people in our congregations are thinking, as well as those who influence them.

We have a great opportunity in predominantly black churches to expand our ministry outreach to those influenced by these false ideologies, but we are going to have to change our playbook to reflect God's heart. We have the gospel and the power of the Holy Spirit to break through the lies of these false ideologies and bring new life to our churches: "Every day the Lord added to their number those who were being saved" (Acts 2:47). The black church is not a substandard spiritual outlet but a part of the universal church that is able to meet these vital needs.

Lament #10: Giving Up on White Christians Who Want to Grow in Their Racial IQ and Contribute to Healing, Resolution, and Restitution

I admit it. There have been times when I've come close to giving up. I don't have time for lingering with those who are unconcerned or apathetic. Even in Jesus' ministry, He didn't waste valuable time with those who chose to live in their fruitless philosophies. Jesus spent the greatest amount of His time with those who may not have understood everything but were willing to endure and grow. Minorities, we must continue to have our hearts and lives open enough to lovingly engage whites who want to grow in their racial IQ. I have been grieved at points in my own journey, but it is unbiblical for me to reject someone who wants to work through issues. I had to decide to spend my energies with those people rather than those who only want to argue and not understand.

There is a growing tendency to respond in ways that do not honor Christ. The way some African Americans communicate on social media concerns me. As a matter of fact, I had to check to make sure I wasn't communicating the same way. They talk about racial injustice but do so in ways that aren't redemptive or helpful. That isn't to say we sugarcoat the message and truth, but we can't stew in bitterness. The writer of Hebrews says, "Pursue peace with everyone, and holiness—without it no one will see the Lord. Make sure that no one falls short of the grace of God and that no root of bitterness springs up, causing trouble and defiling many" (Heb. 12:15). Bitterness is fermented, unrighteous anger and unforgiveness. When we allow bitterness to fester in our hearts, it ends up destroying every area of our lives.

We can't hate our brother and say we love God. For some this is sellout language, but for those who are redeemed, it is the truth. "Whoever claims to love God yet hates a brother or sister is a liar. For whoever does not love their brother and sister, whom they have seen, cannot love God, whom they have not seen" (1 John 4:20 NIV). The truth is not merely what we are to feel, but the truth is what we must obey. Being biblically woke does mean that we hold the majority culture accountable for the racial injustice we are entrenched in. But it also means this is to be done in a spirit of Christian love and with the expectation of redemptive results. To do otherwise will grieve the heart of the living God.

I lament, but I still have hope. My hope is that one day we will rise together, as the people of God, to reclaim our prophetic voice. That is the hope of the Woke Church.

PART THREE

BE ACCOUNTABLE

RECLAIMING OUR PROPHETIC VOICE

In the context of this Biblical tradition we shall not lightly compare—let alone equate—our preaching with prophecy. We are too familiar with the feeble homily, the dull disquisition, the elegant essay, and sometimes, alas, with the impertinences of the pulpit entertainer. But our preaching may have something at least of prophetic quality if we perceive God's presence and his purpose as the decisive factors in the situation in which we and our hearers stand. Our times urgently call for a prophetic word....There is an essential connection between preaching and prophecy, and at times one merges with the other.[1]

PROPHETIC VOICE

When I received my calling into the ministry, I began to look for schools. I didn't know what liberal or conservative was. I looked at the conservative ones, and I was more drawn to them because of their apparent focus on the Bible, exegesis, historical theology, systematic theology, biblical theology, and the biblical languages. In looking at the others, they seemed to focus more on practice. I assumed that the former was more substantive. However, I would learn that no theology or exegesis is done without cultural underpinnings. Liberal schools were honest about this, but the conservative ones I looked into seemed to see their curriculum as culturally neutral.

As I began my studies, I was excited about what I was learning, but I began to observe some cultural gaps between the white students and me. Proclaiming the gospel seemed more cerebral and conversion-centered for them. Anything outside of that was dismissed as "social gospel." Initially, I didn't understand that terminology, but after studying James H. Cone and other theologians, I came to understand what this meant. I found myself exegetically at home with my conservative family on the doctrines of grace, but ethically at home with my liberal family on issues of race and justice. I wasn't comfortable with conservatives' silence on ethical issues during virtually every major wave of injustice in America affecting blacks. But I also balked at liberals and the unclear place of conversion in their teachings.

My theological home of conservative Christianity has become more confusing as the years have gone on. Yet the crumbling ethics of liberal Christianity didn't feel like a solid boat to jump into. So in many ways I have one foot in conservative Christianity and the other foot in liberal Christianity, but I don't feel fully secure in either boat. What would change that for me? If conservatives found a unified prophetic voice. To state it plainly, I'd have to see a significant number of conservative Christians awaken to the far-reaching effects racism continues to have, even in the church.

Prophetic preaching is the bridge between the solid doctrine of conservative Christianity and the Christian ethics of the liberal perspective. Without it, we can easily remain in our own camp, content to cast aspersions and judgments on those on the other side. We desperately need those voices crying in the wilderness making way for His kingdom purposes on earth.

WHAT IS PROPHETIC PREACHING?

Prophetic preaching is the act of the covenant community of Jesus boldly calling all people through the gospel and Word of God back to what it looks like to reflect God's intention for all things. When I say prophetic, I don't necessarily mean foretelling the future, but I'm instead speaking of the *forth telling*. Prophetic preaching is about seeing gaps and calling people to fill them. These gaps are between God's Word and our social-spiritual realities in our world, country, cities, and neighborhoods. Many who hear the term prophetic preaching relegate it to the social justice sphere of preaching. However, Scripture is filled with the prophetic tradition of preaching that reflects God's heart.

Prophetic preaching is big picture visionary preaching that has street-level impact. In essence, it is the urgent call to respond to God individually and collectively. Although prophetic preaching isn't foretelling, it presents the consequences of obedience and disobedience revealed in God's Word. It can even be an invocation of consequences or mercy. A prophetic preacher is biblically soaked and culturally informed.

The prophetic preacher is culturally aware like the tribe of Issachar. The Issacharites understood the times and knew what Israel should do. This tribe had an intimate knowledge of what was going on, but also understood what practical moves the nation needed to make (1 Chron. 12:32). Prophetic preaching also requires being scribal like Ezra: "Now Ezra had determined in his heart to study the law of the LORD, obey it, and teach its statutes

117

and ordinances in Israel" (Ezra 7:10). Ezra studied, applied the Word, and then taught it. That process of study, followed by obedience based on the study, and then teaching, is essential.

The prophetic preacher's message must have certain essentials that distinguish it from a motivational message. It must: contain the gospel, be centered on Jesus, be clear on the issues, be biblically informed, be rhetorically contending, provide visionary hope, and offer clear statements of action.

The Gospel

I know that there has been much prophetic preaching without the gospel. But we need an explicit gospel in the prophetic preaching movement for this hour. When I say the gospel, I mean communicating the content and nature of the gospel. In the words of the apostle Paul: "For I delivered to you as of first importance what I also received: that Christ died for our sins in accordance with the Scriptures, that he was buried, that he was raised on the third day in accordance with the Scriptures" (1 Cor. 15:3–4 ESV). We must have gospel elements in the message, either in whole or in part.

The preached message must address the reality of sin, on an individual level as well as on a systemic level. This is an unpopular notion in a culture where everything is relative and there are no absolutes. But God's Word teaches us—and we know by experience—that all have sinned and come short of the glory of God (Rom. 3:23). That message is more important now than ever before.

And then there is the truth of the gospel. We've already discussed that, but it bears repeating. God, in His matchless grace, took on human flesh to live among sinful men and to die a substitutionary death to pay for all of our sins. Christ died to satisfy the righteous demands of God. And He rose from the dead, providing access to the Father for everyone who would believe in His name. That's the gospel. The cross is the sign that hangs over the head and is planted in the heart of the prophetic preacher. In order to preach with power and stand under the weight of the world's brokenness, we must stand on the stained grounds of the cross. That is why Paul could say, "I decided to know nothing among you except Jesus Christ and him crucified" (1 Cor. 2:2 ESV). Paul prioritized Jesus' sacrificial death when communicating to the Corinthians. And it was under the shadow of the cross that he challenged their party spirit, worldliness, and immorality.

In preaching the cross, one must communicate not only what the gospel is, but also what the gospel *does*. If we say what it is but don't proclaim what it does, then we communicate God's power abstractly. Communicating in prophetic preaching demands saying what the gospel does. In 1 Corinthians 15:3–4 Paul gives the content of the gospel, but in Romans 1:16 he gives the nature of the gospel: "For I am not ashamed of the gospel, because it is the power of God for salvation to everyone who believes, first to the Jew, and also to the Greek." The gospel is the power of God to make changes in people. We must be filled with faith for this as we preach. It isn't just a shouting message; it is a transformational one. There is power in the Word! Without power, what is preaching? You can speak on justice and race with rhetorical excellence, but if the gospel isn't presented, heart change won't happen.

Be Centered on Jesus

We tend to reduce Jesus in the church. He is reduced to a transcendent regenerator, but in the world, He is seen as the eminent social activist/hippie. One side focuses on His individualistic spiritual goals, whereas the other believes He fights the system and leaves our lives alone. One side sees Him as savior of our souls, the other a revolutionary in our culture. One side says, "Just preach the gospel!" The other side says, "Just show the gospel!" Neither is in balance with a comprehensive picture of Jesus. Alone, each view is incomplete.

Prophetic preaching should never separate proclamation and practice. Jesus is the perfect expression of what the gospel is and what the gospel does. The gospel is the message of His redeeming life being poured out in the place of sinners to appease God's wrath. He has been vindicated by being raised from the grave. The gospel message is that God justifies, sanctifies, and glorifies the one who places confidence in Jesus by faith (Rom. 5–8). However, the gospel not only changes the soul and eternal destiny of humans, it also changes brokenness in human relationships and society. That's why Mark calls it the gospel of the Kingdom.

Prophetic preaching must be centered on Christ, "for everything was created by him, in heaven and on earth, the visible and the invisible, whether thrones or dominions or rulers or authorities—all things have been created through him and for him" (Col. 1:16). In other words, Jesus is the producer of all creation. As the creator, He has a right to speak into every aspect of its inner workings. There is nothing we say that can't be traced at its best back to Him. One of His names is the Righteous Judge or the one who Judges Rightly. By His omniscience, He is a witness to everything and His deity makes Him totally objective in judgment. Prophetic preaching that leaves Jesus out isn't preaching; it's just talk.

In Luke 4:17–21, Jesus makes a prophetic kingdom announcement.

> The scroll of the prophet Isaiah was given to him, and unrolling the scroll, he found the place where it was written:

The Spirit of the Lord is on me,
because he has anointed me
to preach good news to the poor.
He has sent me
to proclaim release to the captives
and recovery of sight to the blind,
to set free the oppressed,
to proclaim the year of the Lord's favor.

He then rolled up the scroll, gave it back to the attendant, and sat down. And the eyes of everyone in the synagogue were fixed on him. He began by saying to them, "Today as you listen, this Scripture has been fulfilled."

Luke presents Jesus reading Isaiah 61:1–2a as a prophetic communication and a messianic fulfillment of His purpose. Jesus saw His ministry purpose in Scripture. He saw Himself as empowered by the Holy Spirit in His incarnation as a sign of divine dependence.

He also saw as a mandate the call to proclaim the gospel to the marginalized. "The poor" is a key term in Luke. It refers to the pious poor and indicates Jesus' desire to reach out to those the world tends to forget or mistreat. The purpose of our prophetic voice is to show the world Jesus. Jesus came to show the world the Father by faithfully doing His ministry. We are called to do the same.

Be Clear on the Issues

Prophetic preaching must be clear on the issues of our day. We have to do our homework. In order to appropriately engage the issues, we must know them. There are many glaring issues that need a prophetic voice: classism, sexism, elitism, poverty, ignorance, wealth, greed, etc. We spent a significant portion of Chapter

4 talking about our history of race in America and in the Christian church. Being clear on this issue requires more than just an awareness of our history. We must also examine the impact of our history on our current-day experience. We must ask how this history is still affecting us today. What is the impact of our historical struggle with race on poverty, segregated neighborhoods, and the high concentration of black men in prison?

We must address the things that happen in our culture exegetically, expositionally, theologically, historically, critically, lovingly, passionately, humbly, and with Jesus at the center. To fail to do so is to miss out on our key role as prophetic preachers. I'm not saying that we have to jump at every issue that comes up in the world. However, we should know when an issue reaches a boiling point. It is our job to be in the Word and to soberly assess the world around us.

We are to proclaim the wisdom of God to the seen and unseen authorities. We must speak to causes of suffering and evil, both in the natural and in the spiritual. We don't literally talk to demons and the devil, but the witness of the church in proclamation and practice has power to impact what's behind what we engage on the natural plane. Therefore, preaching is the ultimate Spirit-empowered task. This is the heart of prophetic preaching. It declares God's multidimensional truth to the multilayered challenges in our world that are caused by the enemy's forces. Preaching is spiritual warfare! Ephesians 3:10 tells us that when we preach, something supernatural happens. At the core of prophetic preaching is understanding that we can impact the temporal effects of sin, but also proclaim the coming kingdom of Jesus.

Be Biblically Informed

If we are to regain our prophetic voice, we must have a solid foundation of biblical knowledge and be open to the Spirit's leading in how to apply the balm of God's Word to the issues of our day. In conservative evangelical circles, there has been a resurgence of talk about expository preaching. Expository preaching is driven by the biblical text. David Helm defines expositional preaching as "empowered preaching that rightfully submits the shape and emphasis of the sermon to the shape and emphasis of a biblical text."[2] I love this definition and appreciate the recent emphasis on expository preaching. Yet we can't expect that merely going through the Bible book-by-book will automatically make us relevant. I have preached through multiple books of the Bible, but I also do topical exposition and have found it to be hugely helpful in addressing specific issues.

There seems to be this unwritten rule that anything but book-by-book exposition promotes eisegesis (reading things into the text) or the advancement of personal agendas. In other words, we tend to believe God only uses book-by-book exposition, not topical or doctrinal exposition. In 2 Timothy 4, Paul seems to exhort Timothy to have such a grasp of the Bible that he would be able to preach timely words when people need to hear them. I believe this is still needed today.

Be Rhetorically Contending

The prophets of the Old Testament and the apostles of the New Testament were major contenders. They were bold and aggressive in dealing with those who fought against God's plan for His people. Elijah's standoff against the prophets of Baal is a classic example of contending for the faith (1 Kings 18). Jeremiah contended with the priests and prophets of Judah, boldly proclaiming God's Word: "Then Jeremiah said to all the officials and all the people: The LORD sent me to prophesy all the words that you have heard against this temple and city" (Jer. 26:12).

If we are to regain our prophetic voice, we must contend for the faith against any and every detractor. Like the apostle Paul, we must be able to be bold and unashamed to preach the gospel truth (Rom. 1:16). Our voices are alarmingly quiet in the face of rampant sin and injustice in our culture. We seem to have lost sight of our call to speak truth to power. Where are the Dietrich Bonhoeffers and Martin Luther Kings of our day? Whether the detractors are the political elite, black nationalists, or prosperity gospel proponents, we must engage their false doctrines and ideas and boldly declare the gospel.

I like what Cornel West says: "If your success is defined as being well adjusted to injustice and well adapted to indifference, then we don't want successful leaders. We want great leaders who love the people enough and respect the people enough to be unbought, unbound, unafraid, and unintimidated to tell the truth."[3]

Provide Visionary Hope

Hope is the pillar of the faith that God gives His people so that they can envision change. We believe in a hopeful future because we believe it has been secured by the gospel of Jesus. That is what Dr. King did so well. And that is why the "I Have a Dream" speech resonates with so many people. Though he had not achieved the goals of equal rights, he was able to say, "I've been to the mountain top and mine eyes have seen the coming of the Lord!" That is hope at its best! Anticipation in the midst of challenge! Romans 15:13 has the best statement of hope ever: "Now may the God of hope fill you with all joy and peace as you believe so that you may overflow with hope by the power of the Holy Spirit." What else can you say to that? Prophetic preaching should put this in us. Although we lament, hope is on the other side!

Hope never exists in a vacuum. It produces a love that endures all things. The enduring love that God has for us through the gospel is what keeps us going. We must have enduring love in the body of Christ. Love is what causes those who have been wronged to hold on when letting go is the easy thing to do. Preaching love is the core of the gospel. Enduring with those who have wronged us is the part of the gospel that I sometimes wish wasn't in the Bible. But it is there and must be obeyed. The words of Martin Luther King Jr. help to inspire us and give us much needed hope when we want to quit loving those who wrong us: "Darkness cannot drive out darkness; only light can do that. Hate cannot drive out hate; only love can do that."[4] Prophetic preaching involves explaining what love looks like in action. We have to love when our desired ends have not been met—and we hold on and persevere because our hope lies in Him.

Offer Clear Statements of Action

I have been privileged to share the message of the Woke Church across the country for a few years now. I am encouraged that there is a real desire to know what we, the church, can do to regain our prophetic voice. We will devote an entire chapter to that discussion, but in this space let me suggest that the church—from its beginning—has been known for acting on behalf of the poor and the neglected. The example of the church in Acts 6 in dealing with the issues raised when the Grecian widows were being neglected serves as a template for us today. The church was known for its prophetic care of its members.

We are called to advocate for the poor as an outworking of being a wise covenant community. This is the legacy of the church. Defending the cause of the needy and oppressed is a huge role that we are to be known for as the people of God. It should be an expectation that they have of us and that we have of ourselves.

God's people must function in such a way that we become identified with those who are needy and do not have a voice.

There are many churches that see this as a critical need and
responsibility. The black church, because of its history and formation, saw this as essential for survival.

> In his examination of the economic situation in Afri-
> can American communities, Du Bois concluded that
> any study of "economic cooperation among Negroes
> must begin with the Church group." He was referring
> to the founding and establishment of black churches
> during the period of slavery and in the aftermath of
> the Civil War. Black church members literally pooled
> their pennies and meager resources to buy land to erect
> church buildings in both the North and the South.
> During Reconstruction when many African Americans
> left the plantations or were driven off, they often settled
> in nearby black communities, working as sharecroppers
> on their former master's land or as tenant farmers. These
> communities were often led by their pastors, and their
> churches became the first communally built institutions.
> As the central and dominant institutions in their various
> communities, black churches performed other criti-
> cal roles and functions in the economic sphere to ease
> somewhat the onerousness of abject deprivation.[5]

As a prophetic community, the black church served historically in America as a modern-era, New Testament church. You
can't talk about gospel-centered and Christ-centered ministry
without talking about the black church. Circumstances forced the
black church to look for answers in the Bible and develop a theology that became a robust, comprehensive view of the gospel. The

gospel for the black church was to impact all of life—both soul and the body and the systems in which the disciple found himself. Paul said, "Now may the God of peace himself sanctify you completely. And may your whole spirit, soul, and body be kept sound and blameless at the coming of our Lord Jesus Christ" (1 Thess. 5:23). Paul viewed the spirit, soul, and body as a gateway into the experience of the believer.

What does this have to do with prophetic care? Everything! Judging rightly and treating the poor justly is an outworking of loving your neighbor as yourself. When Jesus was asked about the greatest commandment, he quoted Leviticus 19:18: "Do not seek revenge or bear a grudge against anyone among your people, but love your neighbor as yourself. I am the LORD" (NIV). He saw this as equal to the Shama in Deuteronomy 6:5: "Love the LORD your God with all your heart, with all your soul, and with all your strength."

Pastoring a church in the core of the city places us on the front line in ways that can feel overwhelming. In the beginning, we took these challenges case by case, but as we came into contact with people and began seeing micro cases as a macro problem, we have begun to create systems to be more intentional in our approach. Our goal is for the church to be known to our community and city as a bulwark of kindness.

The chaos in our communities and in our world seems to cry out, "Is there a word from the Lord? Is there manna from heaven to soothe the soul ache of mankind? Is there a balm in Gilead?" The response from a Woke Church that has regained its prophetic voice is a resounding yes! Jesus is still the answer for the world today. I'm praying that God will cause our souls to turn to Him. It is crucial that we engage. And we need Him to help us, first of all, not forget the gospel. We need Him to help us not forget the centrality of Jesus, the might of the cross, and the power of the resurrection to save and transform souls. And we need Him to help us not forget that there are Kingdom implications for everything we do and everything we neglect to do.

A VISION FOR CHANGE

Recently, Meek Mill, a Philadelphia-based rapper who grew up down the street from our church, was incarcerated for a parole violation. He was sentenced to 2–4 years for popping a wheelie on his motorbike in New York. It was clear that the sentence he received was harsh and unfair. I spoke to a member in our church who works as an attorney in the district attorney's office, and the counselor stated that the sentencing was extreme. There was an outcry from the hip-hop community and activists from across the country. Many people said that this over-sentencing is the norm. The unfair sentencing of black men isn't rare. In the case of Meek, information began to surface showing corruption within the system.[1]

The Meek case, and thousands like it, underscores the fact that there's a system of corruption that snares minorities in a trap. Because of the national protest, Meek was released in the end. In the wake of these and many other challenges, the D.A.'s office is working to change faulty laws that impact black men in particular and cause inequitable justice that destroys many lives. The D.A.'s office is considering dropping eight hundred cases that are connected with such corruption. Since Meek is now free, his platform is bringing attention to the challenges of our system and the need for reform.

The church of Jesus Christ must get involved with these challenges facing black men. At its core, this is what it means to be woke. For some readers this isn't new info, but for many this is new and astounding. As incarnational missionaries, we must be woke to brokenness that pervades our society and be a voice for action in these areas. The church should be a leading voice. The writer of Hebrews says, "Remember those in prison, as though you were in prison with them, and the mistreated, as though you yourselves were suffering bodily" (13:3). This scriptural imperative clearly includes those who are unjustly imprisoned.

Hearing these kinds of stories can make the burden seem insurmountable. Every now and then we need the reminder that apart from Him we are nothing. I love the verse in John 15:5 where Jesus says, "I am the vine; you are the branches. The one who remains in me and I in him produces much fruit, because you can do nothing without me." Sometimes we're tempted to think we can live without Him. But we must embrace the fact that we can do nothing without the Lord, especially when we consider how to develop a vision for change in the arena of justice.

Now we're going to talk about an action plan. This is not *the* action plan. This is the vision toward and the foundation for the action plan. It's driven by biblically based, gospel-centered, Jesus-exalting commitment for the church to draft a strategy to help realize shalom in our cities. It will require us to leave the baggage of political and denominational affiliation behind and respond to the call of unity and commitment. This is a vision for change.

The foundation for this action plan comes from an Old Testament passage. (I love exegeting the prophets.) I believe the prophets can show us what it looks like for the gospel to hit the block.

Micah is called a minor prophet, but he has major ideas and concepts in his writings. There was a lot of injustice going on in Israel at the time. The people in Jerusalem had economic wealth but the people in the countryside or the surrounding areas around Judah were living in poverty. So Micah called out the governing authority about its responsibility to address the needs of the poor. He challenged the authorities to go beyond the tower of privilege to the pavement of people's lives.

He began by shining a light on their faulty thinking. "With what shall I come before the LORD, and bow myself before God on high? Shall I come before him with burnt offerings, with calves a year old? Will the LORD be pleased with thousands of rams, with ten thousands of rivers of oil? Shall I give my first-born for my transgression, the fruit of my body for the sin of our soul?" (Micah 6:6-7 ESV). Micah is using hyperbole to show how people think that they can buy their way out of accountability to God. So, he says, you can't tithe your way out of accountability. You can't give the best offering to offset your accountability, to get God off your back. You can't even do what the pagans do and give your kids as an offering. You can't do any of those things. That's not what God is looking for as a viable offering.

God knows you have the money, so money is not really a sacrifice for you. He says, there's something deeper that you need to do in order to sacrifice. He said, "He has told you, O man, what is good; and what does the LORD require of you but to do justice, and to love kindness, and to walk humbly with your God" (Micah 6:8, ESV). That's what He says He wants us to do. I love the fact that He says, "Do justice." I love that He says, "love kindness" (which is an interesting idiom) and "walk humbly with your God."

We've already established that justice is the proper execution of God's laws among God's people. Government officials, based on Romans 13 and 1 Peter 2:14–17, are appointed by God as ministers, whether they're saved or not. This means that God appointed them sovereignly, no matter what happened in the voting booth. Ultimately God appoints leaders for a particular reason. Whether they're good or bad, they'll be held accountable for their actions. But the people of God are supposed to be active and engaging in the midst of all of this.

This vision for change calls the church to pray mightily for the government of our country. Pray for each leader that God has sovereignly put in place. And then speak truth boldly to those leaders without compromise or watering down the message. Believers in the Bible prayed for leaders they disliked. They prayed for them, but then they challenged them about what was right. I like the way John the Baptist did it. John got in front of Herod and blasted him. And Herod said he liked to listen to him (Mark 6:20). He had everybody go out of the room and said, "John's about to talk to me." That's the disposition of a great prophet who's willing to speak into and challenge what's wrong in the culture.

Justice has to be done, not just merely dialogued about. I think we've had more racial reconciliation gatherings than I can count. And when I look at our present—particularly that of black people and ethnic minorities—very little has changed. People have just felt good about getting together, but justice hasn't been done. Therefore, believers have to be energized by the fact that justice is an active part of the gospel. It is not the gospel, but it is an outworking of the gospel.

When Micah says, "and love kindness," love here means to "have a great affection, care for, or loyalty toward something." Kindness is the Hebrew word *hesed* which points to God's loyal love toward us. Loving kindness means that believers are supposed to let the covenant loyalty of God frame their commitment to doing what God calls us to do to engage the inequities in our society.

When you worship and you feel God's presence and those chills go up and down your spine and you tear up because of the presence of the Holy Ghost in the worship gathering and you think about how God provides for you and how He's saved you, it should motivate you to express that *hesed* toward somebody else.

The Christian community shouldn't be a pool; God's called us to be a pipeline. He created us to be a pipeline of grace, mercy, love, and truth. I love it when God does that in our lives, because we know how much we are allowing ourselves to experience the *hesed* of God based on how much we give it out to others.

When we look at this idea of covenant loyalty, of doing justice and loving kindness, it should drive us to act. The Woke Church must be in the business of doing something to stem the tide of injustice in our nation. And I've prepared a framework that encourages action in three categories of justice: Intervening, Preventative, and Systematic. Each type of justice is essential for achieving substantial, long-lasting change, and there are specific activities that both individuals and the church can participate in.

INTERVENING JUSTICE

Anyone who wants to do a comprehensive biblical justice plan must understand how God does justice. This first level of justice is when you go beyond talking to actually practicing and doing what He says. Titus 3 is a beautiful beginning to frame this discussion. Titus 3:1–2 says, "Remind them to be submissive to rulers and authorities, to be obedient, to be ready for every good work, to speak evil of no one, to avoid quarreling, to be gentle, and to show perfect courtesy toward all people" (ESV).

Paul is instructing Titus about the character of God's people in the world. He's reminding him that God's people must be known in the broader community as people who are submissive to those in authority. He's talking about the rulers and authorities in the world—even the unjust ones. We must be known for our obedience and our readiness to do good to others. We must be known for our refusal to speak poorly of others. We must not be contentious. We must be gentle, courteous people. How many of us would say that this is how the church is seen by our world?

So it starts with character. It begins with people who have character and the moral authority to engage. This flows out of the connection to the local church, first. It's not about us doing this on our own. We don't merely do everything that government or those in authority say. When they depart from our biblical convictions, we depart from following them in that particular area. As Peter states in Acts to the governing authorities, "We must obey God rather than men" (Acts 5:29).

Paul talks about spiritual church authority in chapter one of Titus. But then in chapter two, he talks about the nature of Christ's first advent as the means by which the church comes into existence and how discipleship happens. In other words, the church should have its own internal discipleship, but it shouldn't become ingrown. It should engage those outside the ministry.

In verse 14, Paul says, "Let our people learn to devote themselves to good works." He is calling on the church to doing something, not just have meetings and talk. Let them devote themselves to good works so as to help cases of urgent need and not be found unfruitful. If we're not devoted to this, we're missing valuable opportunities to represent Christ in the world.

We must reach into the community and serve the needs of others, but we should approach this with love and humility. We violate Paul's command to speak evil of no one when we see people struggling and, rather than come alongside them, we just blast them on Facebook. We put ourselves in the position of judging another person's choices without understanding what prompted those choices. And then we take all of this out into the public square, sometimes even under the guise of a prayer request. Yet none of this changes the other person's circumstances. Intervening justice calls us to get involved, to come alongside those who are hurting and make a difference.

So where do we see intervening justice in Scripture? Isaiah says, "Isn't this the fast I choose: To break the chains of wickedness, to untie the ropes of the yoke, to set the oppressed free, and to tear off every yoke? Is it not to share your bread with the hungry, to bring the poor and homeless into your house, to clothe the naked when you see him, and not to ignore your own flesh and blood?" (Isa. 58:6–7).

This is what Isaiah is saying. And this is how God wants His people to intervene. You can't help a person who has experienced injustice and a lack of the basic needs of life without first intervening for their current needs. So that means you can't tell them, if they're hungry now, "go get a job." And if they're homeless, you can't tell them to get a job knowing that they don't have any identification or a mailing address.

We can't condemn someone who's on public assistance when we don't know the story of how they got on it. So what we have to do first is learn their story. I know some people who are on public assistance that have degrees. They went through deep times of disability that created a dependence on public assistance. They got trapped in the system. So the most important question is not why did they get trapped, but how can we come alongside them and love on them? You could have been in the position that they're in, if it had not been for God's mercy looking out for you. So, we've got to have intervening justice. If someone needs diapers for her child, we must intervene. If someone doesn't know how to parent, we must intervene. We've got to have intervening justice.

In Matthew 9, we see Jesus' ministry based on this justice

plan. When He came to earth, He didn't come only to die on the cross. Let's look at what He did: "And as Jesus passed on from there, two blind men followed him, crying aloud, 'Have mercy on us, Son of David.' When he entered the house, the blind men came to him, and Jesus said to them, 'Do you believe that I am able to do this?' They said to him, 'Yes, Lord.' Then he touched their eyes, saying, 'According to your faith be it done to you.' And their eyes were opened" (Matt. 9:27–30a ESV).

In verses 32–34, Jesus healed someone who was unable to speak. Then He called the people of God together to talk about the fact that the harvest is plentiful but the laborers are few. He then calls his apostles and sends them out to do what He was doing! "Summoning his twelve disciples, he gave them authority over unclean spirits, to drive them out and to heal every disease and sickness" (Matt. 10:1).

Jesus Christ went and healed diseases. He cast out demons. What is that if it isn't intervening justice? He knew that He couldn't speak of the kingdom to a guy who was deaf. He knew that if He was going to save a guy that couldn't talk, He would have to heal him so he would be able to share his testimony.

In other words, Jesus got involved in real, practical life circumstances of people, and then He tells us to do the same. Jesus didn't come on the scene making systemic change at first. He met immediate needs. I get excited when I think about this. In John 6, the people were hungry, and Jesus fed them because He didn't want to send them home hungry. That was the part of His message—He wanted to communicate His care for them and then to present Himself as the Bread of Life. It's always connected to the gospel! This is a crucial reminder for intervening justice. We must meet needs *and* share the gospel. Without the gospel we are no more than social service agencies.

Intervening justice is up close and personal. It's a response to obvious, prevailing needs. The Woke Church is one that is aware of the urgent needs in its community and does more than just talk about those needs. It marshals its forces to make a difference.

PREVENTATIVE JUSTICE

The second kind of justice is preventative justice. In Mark 11:15–19, Jesus does something interesting. He walks the people of God through a very important lesson. Jesus and the disciples came to the temple. Jesus entered the temple and began to drive out those who were buying and selling (intervention). He overturned the tables of the moneychangers and the seats of those who sold pigeons. And He would not allow anyone to carry anything through the temple (prevention). "He was teaching them: 'Is it not written, My house will be called a house of prayer for all nations? But you have made it a den of thieves!'"(Mark 11:17).

What do we see Jesus doing here? He intervenes, and then He prevents. First he kicks those who are unjustly selling to poor people out of the temple. We learn a key lesson of application here. You can't just have intervening justice and leave people out there. In other words, if you intervene and you just feed them and walk away, you help them to remain in the cycle of continually needing to be fed. However, when we look at the example of Jesus in this particular passage, He teaches us of a greater responsibility.

We have to take preventative measures. This requires the Woke Church to think and pray about ways to get ahead of the issues that confront our communities. Our church wants to have a crisis pregnancy center in the future. But we realize that we can't just have a sonogram machine in there for young ladies to come in and to show them the heartbeat of the children. No, that's not enough. We will need to have biblically based sex education and biblical discipleship of these young women so that we're not just telling them "Don't have sex" or "Here's a condom." We don't do that. That doesn't work, because a condom can't shield you from the wrath of God, even though it can shield you from STDs. We will need to teach them that they are created in the image of God and have worth and dignity and so much more.

The Woke Church is one that will not only be discerning about how to intervene on behalf of the poor and the disadvantaged, but it will also be forward thinking about ways in which it can prevent certain evils from continuing to cause dysfunction in our context.

One of the items on our church's agenda is career path development and entrepreneurial training of those in our community through our Bandwidth program. This program will aid by helping create sustainable economy that stays in the community and reproduces economic growth and wealth. In addition, we have partnered with housing entities who help with down payment assistance and closing costs to encourage home ownership and override redlining in lending in the black community. Each of these is an important preventative step that the Woke Church can take to have a visible, missional presence in the community.

SYSTEMIC JUSTICE

We have intervening justice, preventative justice, and what I call systemic justice. That's the third level. This is where we begin to bring gospel renewal to systems. One of the places we see the biblical mandate for this is in Jeremiah 29:3–7. This is going to help the Woke Church begin to activate and look at systems that need to be challenged and that need the healing that only the gospel can bring.

The Lord clarifies His missional purposes for the people of Israel in Babylon, through His prophet Jeremiah: "Thus says the

LORD of Hosts, the God of Israel, to all the exiles whom I have sent into exile from Jerusalem to Babylon" (Jer. 29:4 ESV). Believers are all exiles, though not in the same way that these Old Testament Jews were. The word "sent" in the Bible is always missiological language. When God sends you somewhere, it's missiological, incarnational language.

So even though the children of Israel are under the discipline of God in this time in their history, God still has them on mission. Even though they're on the outs with the Lord, He still has missiological purpose for them. While they are exiled from Jerusalem to Babylon, He instructs them to

> "build houses and live in them; plant gardens and eat their produce. Take wives and have sons and daughters; take wives for your sons, and give your daughters in marriage, that they may bear sons and daughters; multiply there, and do not decrease. But seek the welfare of the city where I have sent you into exile, and pray to the LORD on its behalf, for in its welfare you will find your welfare."

The word "welfare" there is shalom. Shalom or peace, as I've said before, doesn't mean the absence of conflict. It means the ability to have tranquility and to thrive in the midst of conflict. So when we look at this idea of seeking the peace of the city, shalom means to rebuild things back according to God's original design. And what are some ways we want to do that practically? There are many areas we want to engage: education, history, behavioral sciences, the arts, law and criminal justice, economics, and biblical theology (particularly on race and justice). We'll talk about that in the next chapter.

There are countless systems that need to be impacted by the Woke Church. Education is one of those systems that is close to my heart. It's interesting that even though the children of Israel were in exile, the Babylonians allowed them to be educated in their system. Just like the other Babylonians. Isn't that interesting? They were able to flourish and weren't held back from their ability to maximize their education, even in the midst of captivity.

Nelson Mandela once said: "Education is the great engine of personal development. It is through education that the daughter of a peasant can become a doctor, that a son of a mineworker can become the head of the mine, that a child of farm workers can become the president of a great nation."[2]

I believe that. Our young people are our greatest treasure and responsibility. Every one of them should have a quality education regardless of race or ethnicity. Many young black boys never get the opportunity to stay in school and progress. Many schools have policies in place that push students from the classroom and into the criminal justice system at alarming rates. This is known as the school-to-prison pipeline. Blacks and students with disabilities are disproportionately impacted by these policies:

> Policies that encourage police presence at schools, harsh tactics including physical restraint, and automatic punishments that result in suspension and out-of-class time are huge contributors to the pipeline. But the problem is more complex than that.
>
> The school-to-prison pipeline starts (or is best avoided) in the classroom. When combined with zero-tolerance policies, a teacher's decision to refer students for punishment can mean they are pushed out of the classroom and much more likely to be introduced into the criminal justice system.[3]

One of the things I would love to see is the creation of alternative school options. I'd love to have this happen at Epiphany

Fellowship. I'd love our church to be a place where trained, paid professionals educate kids who fall through the cracks, and then reintroduce them back into the school system. That would require the judge to commit them here to stay and submit to our policies. This is a huge gap that the Woke Church can begin to fill.

We'd also love to provide black teachers who will be able to connect well and motivate the children. In a study done by a John Hopkins economist titled, "With Just One Black Teacher, Black Students More Likely to Graduate," we learn that having "at least one black teacher in third through fifth grades reduced a black student's probability of dropping out of school by 29 percent. . . . For very low-income black boys, the results are even greater—their chance of dropping out fell 39 percent."[4]

Another step in impacting this system in a holistic way is a training program for non-black teachers on how to work with black children. There is a growing body of evidence that "race affects how teachers see and treat their students. Black students taught by white teachers are less likely to be identified for gifted programs than black students taught by black teachers, for example. Other research has shown biases in teachers' grading of work by students of different genders, races and ethnicities."[5]

The Woke Church needs to interrupt the school-to-prison pipeline and speak the gospel into those students' lives. We want to begin to develop relationships and learn people's stories.

The Woke Church is called to three levels of involvement and action: intervening justice, preventative justice, and systemic justice. May God help us to engage at each level of justice, proclaiming His truth to the darkness and righteously acting on His command to seek the welfare of the city.

PART FOUR

BE ACTIVE

THE WOKE CHURCH
IN ACTION

As I have been privileged to share this message of the Woke Church across the country, I have been encouraged by the requests to know how we can move forward. What should we do? The following suggestions are just a sampling of the many ways that we can bring intervening, preventative, and systemic justice to our communities.

IMAGO DEI AS FOUNDATIONAL BIBLE DOCTRINE

From the lack of diverse racial representation in superheroes stories to Christian movies to homeschooling curriculum, there is a pressing gospel need to demonstrate the dignity of each individual. My oldest son is a great artist. He began sketching at a pretty young age. I noticed that his characters were always white, even when he created superheroes. I finally asked him, "Son, what color do you wish you were?" He said, "White!" As we worked through this issue, it was obvious that he had been impacted by the images of whiteness that he had experienced over the years. From that point on, my wife and I wanted him to experience both positive black images and global culture as he grows to love the person God created him to be.

Imago Dei must become a key part of the foundational biblical and gospel education for all believers. Just as the Jerusalem Council clarified the issues that were to be foundational Christian education and practice for Gentiles, so the Western church needs to value people as created in the image of God. That should be core to our teaching. We need to constantly remind ourselves that, because of our history in this country, we often don't readily see that we are all created in the image and likeness of God. As we teach creation, fall, redemption, and consummation, we must zoom in on human dignity in the creation section of the classes and discipleship. We must repent of the teachings that the church has overtly and covertly communicated about blacks in the narrative and theology of American history. Because there was Christian participation in creating false doctrines about black humanity, we must have open dialogue and repentance about this until these false ideas are eradicated from Christianity.

Tony Evans engages this well in *Oneness Embraced*:

> On one side, I was being told that I was created in the image of God and therefore had value. On a pragmatic basis, however, it appeared to me that the benefits of possessing that divine image were reserved for white people because it seemed that they were the real benefactors of God's kingdom on earth.[1]

This sentiment cannot be the sentiment in the church. In our membership classes, theological education, disciple making, pastoral search committees, we must emphasize God-given dignity.

LISTENING TO AND LEARNING ONE ANOTHER'S STORIES

I encourage majority-culture churches to find an ethnic minority church in your region, and humbly say to them, "We want to come to the table. We want to understand what's going on." We increase our racial IQ by getting around people that can help us with that. Time can be spent bringing up issues that have happened in the culture and sharing with each other how those issues impact our communities. It's important to share with one another to hear our stories. But I would also say that we don't build relationships with one another in order to have a mission field. You build a relationship with a person because you want to know them, love them, and do life with them . . . and out of that can come healing.

This is best experienced in the context of hospitality on both a corporate and individual level. Soong-Chan Rah explains this well:

> In the context of the Ancient Near East, the value of hospitality cannot be overemphasized. "In a number of ancient civilizations, hospitality was viewed as a pillar on which all morality rested." In the Old Testament, we see examples of the lack of hospitality being the equivalent of a blatant insult.
>
> We see the sense of responsibility that individuals in these times and places felt to offer hospitality, often at great costs. We see the call for hospitality in the ministry of Jesus in how an itinerant, essentially homeless rabbi offers hospitality at the messianic banqueting table in feeding thousands. . . . Early Christian writers claimed that transcending social and ethnic differences by sharing meals, homes, and worship with persons of different backgrounds was a proof of the truth of the Christian faith.[2]

Hospitality is a major tool to build an environment of relationship and understanding. God has created a people from all people, and, therefore, expects us to function accordingly. I have experienced this on many occasions. Whenever this happens, it usually proves powerful for all those who are involved in the experience of hospitality as we hear one another's stories and understand why we are where we are today.

On one such occasion at Harvey and Rachael Turner's home in Reno, Nevada, they invited a group of leaders from all over the globe for dinner. There were European and non-European whites, African Americans, Latinos, and Asians present. By the fire pit that night, we had amazing conversation and were able to all grow an inch or two closer by just being together as brothers and sisters in Jesus listening and learning from one another. We laughed, cried, yelled, and whispered all evening. Days after that time together we all affirmed that it was one of the most helpful times we had ever experienced as we talked through issues. To hear about race in Ireland and Scotland and the Latino community and in the African American experience was amazing. We learned so much from one another and have continued the dialogue since then. Rachael will randomly text my wife about what she's up to and how it is affecting her view of the racial issues in America. Harvey has made significant adjustments in his church through staffing and church planting.

The church at large should always have a learning disposition— learning about our communities' needs, thinking, brokenness, strengths, cultural make up, challenges, communication, media habits, etc. Many churches have died because of the lack of foresight to break through the walls of their building to meet and engage the people they drive and walk past week after week. At Epiphany, we have many people that live in the community going to the church, but we also have many from the city and surrounding region.

In light of this, as a pastor, I don't assume anything. I know that I must be constantly working to remain aware of what is happening in the neighborhood and throughout the surrounding community.

Our church has done this through our prayer walks. We use the first Sundays of the month to venture into our neighborhood to pray, learn, and share the gospel. We have been able to deepen our heart for our community just based on these regular interactions to build awareness. When I train leaders in urban environments in particular on this, they are blown away at how much they see when they are out on their feet, beating the pavement instead of driving. Walking slows you down, and you have to face people eye to eye. Yes, we have been cursed out and threatened before, but overall people are very surprised that the church would even attempt to hear from them.

ENHANCED THEOLOGICAL EDUCATION

I've already shared my belief that the theological academy needs to broaden the borders of historical theology. We don't want to paint history black but be honest about all ethnicities and particularly the contributions of people of color in biblical history. We need textbooks that reflect truth concerning biblical history. The images used should display the richness and diversity of our faith. Practical theology classes need to be developed that focus on the needs in black, poor, and middle-class spheres. We must help people understand how the Bible addresses key questions concerning dignity, identity, and significance. Graduates who have this base of knowledge will be well equipped to serve the Lord in practical ways in urban ministry.

The skewing of biblical history that omits the contributions of people of color has a direct impact on the students who attend Christian schools. In many cases, black students who attend evangelical schools come out less equipped to minister to black people than when they went in! Many of these young graduates end up in white churches or unable to connect to a local church community that may have a significant black population. In the worst cases, some of these students graduate with a disdain for the black church.

FACING OUR BLIND SPOTS AND APATHY

As I have spoken in recent years on race at several conferences and churches, I've heard one statement repeatedly: "Why do we have to keep talking about this?" The question is evidence of a level of disconnectedness that is either willful or based on a lack of knowledge. This is what apathy looks and sounds like. It's a luxury for those who live on the other side of injustice and racism. It stems from a perspective that says, *this doesn't have anything to do with me.* That statement couldn't be further from the truth. An injustice done to one human being is an injustice done to us all. Each injustice seeks to weaken the fabric of our humanity and must be resisted at all costs.

Racial injustice is not restricted to America; it's a worldwide concern. We can learn from other nations that have taken major steps and have experienced great fruit in honestly looking at their past in an unfiltered way. From Rwanda's Gacaca Court to South Africa's Reconciliation Committee to Germany's De-Nazification Program—each country created systemic ways to educate and restitute the wrongs of their past. The church could use these as a model for how we can become a practical prophetic community. Let's take a closer look at each.

The word "Gacaca" refers to "a bed of soft green grass." In ancient traditions, it was where "a community and its representatives, mainly elders, leaders and individuals known for their integrity and wisdom, gathered to discuss and resolve conflicts within [the village]. . . . The Gacaca called upon the accused families or person to reconcile with the complainant, and vice versa. This conflict resolution system's origins could be traced back to the 15th century when the kingdom of Rwanda became more socially and politically organized."[3] The Gacaca courts played a significant role in finding out the truth of what happened during the genocide against the Tutsi. They allowed communities across Rwanda to meet, face to face, and talk about the events of 1994. In this way, they laid the foundation for peace and reconciliation.[4]

In South Africa, the Reconciliation Committee was set up by the Government of National Unity to help deal with what happened under apartheid. The conflict during this period resulted in violence and human rights abuses from all sides. No section of society escaped these abuses. A key part of their national healing began with the Truth & Reconciliation forums where each side shared what they had experienced with the other. They formed a Human Rights Violation Committee, Reparations and Rehabilitation Committee, and an Amnesty Committee to ensure that victims were being served well on several levels.

Germany has a de-nazification program meant to purge Germany of the remnants of Nazi rule and rebuild its civil society, infrastructure, and economy. The program included compulsory visits to nearby concentration camps and the viewing of films documenting the Nazis' treatment of "inferior" people. This program is based on the truth that seeing is believing.

> Often the only thing capable of denting humanity's
> monumental ability to hunker down in a state of denial
> is indisputable, visual evidence. When cruel things take
> place on a massive and institutionalized scale behind
> closed doors and out of sight in societies, only jarring

151

confrontation can shatter the delusions. "If the ear won't listen, tell it to the eye."[5]

The healing in each of these countries was based on an accurate understanding of the truth. In our reeducation and effort toward reconciliation and justice, the church must work to fill the truth gaps concerning the reality of our past and present. The Evangelical Covenant Church offers the Sankofa Journey, which provides a cross-racial prayer journey for Christians to learn about the history of racism in our country. It's an interactive experience that tours historic sites of importance during the Civil Rights movement and sites of oppression for people of color, while seeking to move participants toward healing the wounds and racial divide caused by hundreds of years of injustice.[6] This can be an invaluable step in moving forward.

The church in America has a great advantage in these matters. We have the empowering of the Holy Spirit to guide us, and we can learn from the experiences of other nations that have gone before us to tackle this extremely difficult issue.

THE CHURCH AS A FAMILY TRAINING CENTER

The psalmist said, "Unless the LORD builds a house, its builders labor over it in vain" (Ps. 127:1). As the NET Bible notes, "The expression *build a house* may have a double meaning here. It may refer on the surface level to a literal physical structure in which a family lives, but at a deeper, metaphorical level, it refers to building, perpetuating, and maintaining a family line. See Deut 25:9; Ruth 4:11; 1 Sam 2:35; 2 Sam 7:27; 1 Kgs 11:38; 1 Chr 17:10, 25. Having a family line provided security in ancient Israel."[7] The biblical concept of a family line has powerful application for the gospel theology of dignity for our day. Willie Richardson, in his book *Reclaiming the Urban Family,* offers a number of reasons why the church needs to be a family training center and how the church is uniquely equipped to do this, including: 1) "The church represents God in the world"; 2) "God is the creator of marriage and family"; 3) "The church has been commissioned to reach the world for Christ"; 4) "The church has received agape love (God's love) to dispense to others in need"; 5) "The church is the embassy that houses Christ's ambassadors"; and 6) "The church is involved with people from birth."[8]

The church is called to bring the light of the gospel to impact the rising tide and the impact of drugs in urban areas. As crime increases, fear and death do too. Families struggle with how to survive and remain stable with such strong influences. The church of Jesus Christ is uniquely equipped to speak into this deep need.

Tony Evans says:

> In our society today, many of our families have a foundation problem. Because of this, the majority of them are spending their time dealing with the cracks on their walls. They are trying to plaster over and patch up an argument here, or a fight there, or deal with rebellious children, or any number of things. But they spend all of their time and money focusing on the fissures rather than solidifying the foundation. Because of this there is family chaos in our world.[9]

The family is the foundation of our communities. When they are destroyed, our communities fail. They cease to be nurturing places. We must minister directly to these needs and get rid of any ministry that is a distraction to this within our churches.

Out of robust family ministry comes a community of spiritual mothers and fathers. These spiritual parents bring an understanding of the gospel and biblical community. As this gospel family grows as a community of faith that is committed to restoring dignity through the gospel, generational dignity increases and the church is woke to the larger societal issues of race and justice.

Biblical Womanhood Training

> In the same way, older women are to be reverent in behavior, not slanderers, not slaves to excessive drinking. They are to teach what is good, so that they may encourage the young women to love their husbands and to love their children, to be self-controlled, pure, workers at home, kind, and in submission to their husbands, so that God's word will not be slandered. (Titus 2:3–5)

God's Word provides a clear mandate for older, mature women in the church to teach/train younger women the principles of biblical womanhood. The black church was revolutionary in developing dignity through programs, awards, and celebrations for black girls. They created enrichment programs including, but not limited to, black history studies, oratorical contests, fashion shows, drama productions, educational trips, mentoring, tutoring, youth retreats, Bible memorization competitions, inviting successful black women speakers, and volunteering. The black church did what the public school didn't do, and what poor parents couldn't afford to do because most enrichment programs for girls were costly and designed for whites or the middle class. It was the hands-on attention and cheers of the black church that sowed seeds of dignity for girls. The black church told girls they were pretty, smart, and important. The church needs to return to these key roles and functions.

The lack of a father figure in the lives of some black women—

particularly young singles—can leave them feeling exposed and vulnerable, without a sense of shelter, guidance, or protection. Widows, the elderly, single parents, and divorcees need practical help with finances, parenting, housing, transportation, and legal issues. The church needs to formalize and publicize ministries of care that serve the multifaceted needs of these women.[10]

Black women who receive seminary training have an uphill battle because many churches don't have a vision for how to use their extraordinary talent. My wife and I have female friends who have seminary degrees and have found it difficult to find work because many churches lack a vision to see women beyond traditional roles. It is incumbent on leadership to reevaluate areas where women have been relegated to serve that are not based on biblical prohibitions but rather on cultural practices that may be extensions of sexism and misogyny. Black women should be affirmed to serve in greater capacities than the traditional roles of children's ministry, choir, and hospitality.

The goal is to release women for expanded Titus 2 and Great Commission mandates. Women can serve communion, teach in appropriate settings, lead ministries and small groups, be theologians, professors, apologists, deacons, evangelists, and missionaries, read Scripture, pray in public, be involved in social justice, develop curriculum, provide counseling, be trained for leadership, work on church staff, and speak on various platforms where they should be compensated like male speakers.[11]

Biblical Manhood Training

If any church is going to be woke, it must seek to develop men who reflect robust masculinity and visionary leadership for the family. Manhood training is the God-given leading edge for restoring black dignity.

In my book, *Manhood Restored: How the Gospel Makes Men Whole*, I talk about how important it is for men to be real men. "Paul implemented manly men as the earliest church leaders. He left Timothy in Ephesus to challenge men who were destroying the work of the gospel in church. In 1 Timothy 1:3, Paul tells Timothy to charge or order the men who are dominating the teaching with false teaching. This kind of confrontation would require a manly man, one unafraid to confront issues head-on and face-to-face."[12]

These are the kind of men that the church needs to be raising up now. Strong men who are able to model biblical manhood for our boys and challenge the evils of the culture that threaten to swallow them up. There are a number of quality programs that churches can engage in to teach manhood. Of them, "33: The Series" is one that I highly recommend. It's "a multi-volume video series that gives men a vision for manhood as modeled by Jesus in His 33 years on earth."[13] The lessons for men on design, story, work, traps, marriage, and fatherhood are invaluable.

There is an attack on the black male on every front. From mass incarceration, under-education, social and psychological genocide, and self-hatred, black men experience an attack. We must find ways for the church to engage these dire issues.

Challenge the Criminal Justice System

God's church must challenge an appalling injustice—the pattern of black men being given harsher sentences than our white counterparts. "Although the majority of illegal drug users and dealers nationwide are white, three-fourths of all people imprisoned for drug offenses have been black or Latino. In recent years, rates of black imprisonment for drug offenses have dipped somewhat, declining approximately 25 percent from their zenith in the mid-

1990s." But African Americans remain "incarcerated at grossly disproportionate rates throughout the United States."[14]

Philadelphia Eagles' quarterback Malcolm Jenkins illustrated this reality in a silent interview with reporters. They would pose a question to him about the team visiting the White House, and he would hold up a sign: "More than 60% of people in prison are people of color." They would ask another question, and he would hold up a sign saying, "You aren't listening!" In many ways it seems that few people are listening and paying attention to these gross inequalities.

Epiphany's Woke Church legal guild is looking at mass incarceration with our educational team. We want to help engage the school-to-prison pipeline in our city. Every church should engage this in a way that is manageable, with outside partners who have strengths and connections that exceed our own.

The church of Jesus Christ must work on intervention and prevention. We must develop after-care programs for those coming out of the system. When possible we should find ways to help those who qualify have their records expunged. Our church had the privilege of helping a young man get his record cleared. The young man is doing well, working in a viable self-employed job, and is married and has bought a home. We are so grateful for this.

On the prevention end of engagement, we must advocate for equal and just sentencing. We had the opportunity to become involved in the case of a fifteen-year-old young man. He was arrested for looking like a suspect. He was placed in general population without a formal case or legal judgment for almost a year. He spent his sixteenth birthday in prison. He may never be the same because the environment in the prison hardened him. Other young men in our ministry who have had a negative relationship with the law find themselves more married to the street life after being released from juvenile detention centers. The church's voice must get in front of this by finding specific ways to speak out as a united entity apart from the system and develop appropriate partnerships that don't get highjacked by other agendas.

Develop Community Partnerships

Partner with churches and parachurch ministries that have a healthy connection to local churches and have a sustainable vision for gospel transformational ministry in places of systemic need. These types of partnerships will prove beneficial for the people we serve, and those we partner with.

I've seen God work mightily through these relationships. Partnership in the gospel is an extremely helpful way to build relationships across ethnic lines. At Epiphany we have forged relationships that have spanned a decade, and I believe all parties would attest that these partnerships have been mutually beneficial.

I have had a friendship with Matt Chandler and the Village Church for over a decade. It started as a relationship that centered around the Village Church partnering with us for planting. But it all began with the two of us building relationship. Our friendship and partnership grew over the years, from preaching for each other (a lot), connecting our families, and serving on the board of Acts 29 together. As the years have progressed, many of Matt's church members have expressed their appreciation for how my relationship with him and their church has affected their journey in the gospel. Matt and Lauren are dear friends and ministry partners. We are family.

Leverage Our People Resources

Many times churches, from small to large, possess great people resources. Even if you are in a place where there aren't many African Americans, you can reach out to predominantly non-white churches and ask, "How can we come alongside a project or solution that will help advance and serve the vision God has given you?" Consider the resources in your church. Are there retired teachers, coaches, and financial planners? Are there business people who can be stirred to provide business training?

I have had to work to raise a good bit of money over the years for urban ministry, and those who have provided resources already had a sense of what I was about doctrinally and missiologically prior to partnership. There can be ongoing ways that you partner and build relationships that will help heal wounds through gospel restitution and will help build common ground for the gospel in massive ways.

Here's one example: Matt Chandler's Village Church had a member who found out that we needed a playground on our property. Through this man's playground building business, he donated playground equipment worth tens of thousands of dollars in our neighborhood where the average household income is $15,000. When the crew was building it, neighborhood residents, including local Muslim residents, couldn't believe that a church was doing this. The builder wanted to make sure that the Lord and the church got credit, not him. For many in our community it increased the church's credibility. Many daycare centers and schools in our community use it for their recess space. Kids play a lot out there, and neighbors view it as their playground, not just Epiphany Fellowship's. We named it Diamond Street Community Park to reinforce the idea that it belongs to the community, not just the church.

Create Spheres for African-American Discipleship and Missiology

Although we are all family cross-ethnically in the church, many non-white groups feel like their unique cultural needs aren't being met. The Body of Christ is one body, but we are not monolithic. We are comprised of diverse groups with specific needs and challenges.

One of the reasons we started our Thriving program was to provide a place for minorities to be able to address our ministry needs and collaborate on solutions. Much of the feedback we have received has been very helpful. As a resource collaborative, we want to see ministry in the urban context go from surviving to thriving. My friends Bryan Loritts and Blake Wilson have accomplished this with Kainos Movement and with Mannafest. The Jude 3 Project, led by Lisa Fields, is committed to equipping the local Church in fulfilling the mandate of Jude 13—contend for the faith that was once for all entrusted to God's holy people. We can be unapologetically Christ-driven and unapologetically black, without being seen as separatist.

I believe that if we will all support one another in love for these distinct needs to be met, we will find more unity. Acts 15 is about understanding and supporting ethnic distinction and mission in different contexts without losing the centrality of the gospel. The Gentiles were encouraged to know that, although they were in a different location in God's vineyard, they had an equal faith with the Jerusalem church. The Gentile believers were given specific instructions to help them be sensitive to their Jewish brethren and maintain the unity of the body. By sending the letter, the Jews were saying that they acknowledged the Gentile faith and saw this as a way to make sure that they remained unified, although they were in different mission fields. As Christians in this era, we must mutually affirm our unity without seeing our different mission field needs, and how those needs are met, as divisive.

WOKE CHURCH THINK TANK

We began an initiative at Epiphany Fellowship that I pray can serve as a model for how churches can aid deeply in areas of great need in our city and others across the country. It is called the Woke Church Interdisciplinary Think Tank. The Think Tank exists to mobilize those with professional skills to employ their expertise for gospel change in the world. Our desire is to engage issues of justice in our neighborhood and encourage it abroad as well. Currently, our primary areas of focus include:

> Health—In the area of health, we deal with female crisis pregnancy through a partnership with several crisis pregnancy outlets. One is Alpha Care. Every Monday they provide crisis pregnancy care at Epiphany Fellowship. In addition, in our community outreaches they provide consultation and share the gospel with those we connect with during events.

> Behavioral sciences—This part of the initiative is still in its infancy, but the goal is to have trained sociologists and psychologists working through how the church can engage generational trauma and understand the ethos of the community as we engage the invisible systems that exist in cities. By invisible systems I mean key issues of suffering and social challenge that don't get exposed and aided outright. For instance, several of our social workers lived and worked in the neighborhood. They were able to give us commentary on sexual brokenness, mental illness, and family dysfunction that goes over the heads of the city and the churches. We aren't trying to solve every issue, but we want to understand what shapes the dysfunction and how to engage it in our sphere.

Education and history—Our educational guild is made up of educators and administrators from the elementary level through college. Right now we are trying to connect with the schools that we, as a church, work in. We're trying to fight the school-to-prison pipeline. We're engaged in increasing the awareness of this problem and how it has become a systemic issue. We provide dictionaries for schools that can't afford them and look forward to developing a library in a school that lacks a viable library. We are excited about taking this initiative to encourage literacy and look forward to stocking the library with books that are culturally sensitive.

Economics—We want to help create more black businesses in our neighborhood beyond barbershops and beauty salons. We have designed our Bandwidth Technology Institute to help with this pressing need. This institute will help train business owners in our city and community to build sustainable businesses that create jobs within the community itself. Individuals will learn everything from coding, to business plan development, to how to raise start-up capital.

Community outreach—At Epiphany Fellowship we have three levels of engagement: blitzes, connecting events, and city investment. City investment is more long-term yet sustainable programs that we do to help where there are gaps. We began a basketball league in our church. Although there are other leagues, that league became a significant activity for our neighborhood and city. We found out that one of the schools that we are mentoring in had their sports programs cut.

Without us knowing it, our basketball league became
the sports program for that school.

For us, the kingdom coming to our city is proclaiming the
good news of Jesus, meeting pressing needs, and building common ground for gospel engagement.

JOINING SWORDS

As I grieved the increasing racial injustice in our country, a
white pastor friend of mine sent me a text that said, "My sword is
yours!" It was refreshing to hear from a brother in Christ, wanting to help address the systemic problems in our country. I've
said much about ways in which the church can respond with intervening, preventative, and systemic justice. In some ways, this
may feel overwhelming. It might feel like it's too much, almost
impossible. It can be boiled down to a pretty simple statement.
*What needs to happen in the body if we are going to work together
cross-ethnically is that white Christians must reach across the color
line and begin building respect and trust for minorities. Minorities
must respond with open arms and hearts to these efforts.*

MSNBC hosted a panel discussion on "Everyday Racism in
America." One of the powerful points of action that was recom-
mended: whites need to speak up whenever they see something
that looks like racism and injustice. We would be light years
ahead if minorities weren't the only ones talking about racism. A
recent event at a Starbucks that resulted in the company closing
every one of its stores in America for racial sensitivity training
was in response to whites who became outraged at the unfair
treatment of two black men in a Philadelphia Starbucks. These
kinds of occurrences happen every day. As Christians, it is our
responsibility to stand up and speak out.

These action points are not comprehensive. They are meant to spur the Woke Church to action—to help us become instruments of justice in our world. Nothing is accomplished without someone taking the first step and initiating the first action. Ask God where He wants you to begin, as a church and as an individual, to make your mark for the cause of the gospel. And then find a friend or another church to partner with in this great work. This is the work of the Woke Church! And the work of the Woke Church is preparing us for a future that is glorious!

9

SEEING THROUGH THE LENS OF THE END

When I went to grad school, I was hit with syllabus shock. We had to read thousands and thousands of pages of text. I had to learn terms I had never heard before: evangelical, fundamentalism, hypostatic union. We had to learn about all of the Councils. One professor even gave us tests on footnotes. For a few years, I was in a daze. I was lost and confused, and it all seemed meaningless. But when I began spending time with the Bloods and the Crips and learning how to share the gospel, everything started to look different. At first, grad school was just something to get through. It was something to survive. But as I saw that my education was bigger than verb tenses in Hebrew—that it was literally preparing me to do the work of the gospel—I began to see the bigger picture. When you get a perspective on the bigger picture, minutiae have depth. The everyday experience of getting my lessons done began to make sense. I had flourished in my work because I had seen the bigger picture.

A lot of what we have talked about in this book has been heavy. I know it has. These are weighty matters. The work of the Woke Church can seem tedious and meaningless. It can be especially hard to stand in the face of opposition when you're just trying to do justice and to love people. You may be tempted to give up and return to business as usual, unless you've seen the bigger picture. The bigger picture makes it all worthwhile. It puts all of the sacrifices into perspective and energizes the work. And that's what I want to leave you with—a vision of the bigger picture. I want us to look to the end and be reminded of where we're all headed. I really believe that should inform our view of everything we're dealing with right now.

Growing up in the black church, I was keenly aware of our focus on the bigger picture, the glorious end of it all. If you want to know a church's theology, just listen to what it sings. I remember singing that old hymn, "We're Marching to Zion":

Come, ye that love the Lord, and let your joys be known,
Join in a song with sweet accord, join in a song with sweet accord.
And thus surround the throne, and thus surround the throne.
We're marching to Zion, beautiful, beautiful Zion;
We're marching upward to Zion; the beautiful city of God.
Then let our songs abound and every tear be dry;
We're marching through Immanuel's ground;
we're marching through Immanuel's ground,
To fairer worlds on high, to fairer worlds on high.
We're marching to Zion, beautiful, beautiful Zion;
We're marching upward to Zion; the beautiful city of God.

I have grown and am still growing in this song's eschatological depths. As one of my favorite call to worship songs, it was an awesome reminder that the struggles of this life will pale in comparison to what heaven has in store for the believer. Songs like "Trouble Don't Last Always" and "Thank You, Lord" show us that our music is both transcendent and imminent, now and futuristic. Life can be difficult now, but the return of Jesus gives hope for today and a passion for tomorrow. It is impossible to talk about race and injustice without having in mind what the future holds for the church. We need to have a biblical worldview on all that is happening today, with an eye always on our glorious future. If we believe that Christ is going to come back and put everything under His feet, that means our view of race, our view of ethnicity, our view of everything must be informed by God's Word and not our feelings. We hold our present circumstances up against the knowledge that race, ethnicity, and justice are all going to look different when Jesus comes back. Our future is bright and we are moving towards unity.

The apostle John in Revelation 7:9–17 gives us a picture of our promised future. There is a revolution coming. But this revolution will not happen without the eternal revolutionary, the God-Man Jesus Christ.

> After this I looked, and there was a vast multitude
> from every nation, tribe, people, and language, which
> no one could number, standing before the throne and
> before the Lamb. They were clothed in white robes
> with palm branches in their hands. And they cried out
> in a loud voice:
>
> Salvation belongs to our God,
> who is seated on the throne,
> and to the Lamb! (vv. 9–10)

Eschatology means "last things." It doesn't matter whether you're pre-millennialist, post-millennialist, amillennialist, pre-trib, or mid-trib. . . . Revelation isn't about any of those things. What Revelation is about is The Revelation of Jesus Christ. This passage is a portal, a passage into the future. John is imprisoned on the island of Patmos. He's alone. Many other followers of the faith have been martyred. An angel comes to him in a vision and takes him on a journey. It's like "A Christmas Carol." The angel takes him through things past, things present, and things to come. He brings him to earth and shows him a mess. Then he takes him to heaven. Earth is such a mess that the angel has to hurry up and take John to heaven to see what things are going to be like, so he won't be discouraged. If John needed help and some perspective to understand all that was happening, how much more do we need it?

My mother loved to read the book of Revelation to me. She'd say, "Now baby, people are getting real crazy. You better read the Bible and figure out what's going on." The truth is that the Bible says it only gets worse before it gets better. We can't let these issues of race make us forget that Jesus is coming back. We may think anger, and picketing, and legislation, and hashtags change things. But there's a real revolution coming. He will set all things in order.

John is discouraged when he sees what will happen on earth. But his mind is blown when he sees heaven. He sees a great multitude that no one can number. This is a fulfillment of the Abrahamic covenant when God said, "all the peoples on earth will be blessed through you" (Gen. 12:3). What I like about this is that it is not Jewish seed. This is global seed. This is everybody—past, present, and future—who has been redeemed and brought into the family of God. How do we know that?

EVERY NATION, EVERY TRIBE, ALL PEOPLES, ALL LANGUAGES

John says they are "from every nation, from all tribes, all peoples, and all languages." How did they get there? Over time, because of Christ's death and resurrection, somebody had to tell folks about Jesus. Scripture asks, "How can they hear without a preacher?" (Rom. 10:14). And Jesus said that He wouldn't set up His kingdom until this gospel has been preached in all the world for a witness to all nations. (Matt. 24:31). That means every tribe, every language, every nation is there.

In order to bring ultimate reconciliation between the races, somebody had to focus on God instead of merely themselves. Somebody had to cross into a time zone and a people group that was unfamiliar. Somebody did church planting; somebody did outreach. Some women walked in biblical femininity; some men walked in biblical masculinity. Some professors used their platform to preach the gospel. Some business people used their platform to preach the gospel. Some counselors slid Jesus in when the door opened. Somebody on the block shared the gospel with somebody else. Like the Wycliffe Bible translators, somebody went somewhere, learned the language, and then translated the Scriptures into that new language—there was some cross-ethnic sacrifice. Somebody made a sacrifice for others to hear the gospel.

And in Revelation, they're all before the throne. It says every nation. This is every single nationality of people that has ever existed, even the extinct ones. Even before the ethnicities got mixed. All of these people are before the throne of God praising Him in languages.

"From one man he has made every nationality to live over the whole earth and has determined their appointed times and the boundaries of where they live" (Acts 17:26). Here, Paul is saying that God has placed people in every ethnicity that exists.

That means whatever you are ethnically, God placed you. You are not here by accident. God singled you out and created you for a purpose. In heaven we will be ethnically and personally distinguishable. We won't turn into some unified color consciousness. We will be able to be personally seen.

To say it plainly, God does care about color and ethnicity. Revelation and the Bible itself show us that God values our color and ethnicity because He created it. We will maintain our ethnicity whether mixed, black, brown, yellow, red, olive, or white—our distinctions will be distinct yet unified under the eternal Lordship of Jesus. And the reason He singled you out is so that He could have representation of your people group in heaven! Ethnicities are the beauty of God's manifold grace being displayed in the pantheons of His power so that people can see and honor and lift Him up.

John sees a multitude that represents not only every nation, every tribe, and every people, but also every language. God actually created languages. When the people of God tried to build the Tower of Babel, God decided to confound their languages (Gen. 11:1–9). They were trying to get big. He already knew what they were doing, but He said, "Let's go down there" (v. 7). He looks at them, confounds their languages, and causes confusion. They can't understand each other anymore so they spread out across the earth, and God used that for His glory. He spread out the people so there could only be union in Him.

Then on the Day of Pentecost, He used what pushed people away from each other to bring them together again. He gave all of those people one Spirit, so that even though they were speaking in different languages to the glory of God, everyone heard in their native tongue.

Standing in His Presence

Then John is transported to the third heaven, and sees the Lord Jesus. And the peoples and nations are standing before a throne. There is a plurality of people, but only one throne. They are before the throne and the Lamb. All of these ethnicities are before God the Father and God the Son, and God the Spirit fills everybody. God the Father is at the left of Jesus Christ, emanating from His excellence and His glory.

The Bible says that God dwells in unapproachable light (1 Tim. 6:16). Jesus Christ the Lamb is present and ushering the saints into God's presence, so God's presence won't destroy us as we dwell in that unapproachable light. And please notice that we're standing. When you come into a king's throne room, the first thing you do is bow down. But something is strange in this text: everybody at this point is standing. The psalmist posed the question, "Who may stand in his holy place?" (Ps. 24:3). Yet here we're seeing the equality of all people who have been washed by the blood of the Lamb and made worthy through Christ to be able to stand before God. They're not standing in themselves; they're standing in the Lamb. They're not proclaiming how great they are or what they did for Christ. They're standing and they're showing how worthy Christ is!

United in Praise

The people are clothed in white robes that have been washed in the blood of the Lamb, and they are holding palm branches. Palm branches point to a victory celebration! According to Craig Keener, "Palm branches celebrated the victory of Israel's exodus from Egypt, and the feast commemorated God's faithfulness to them during their wanderings in the wilderness, when they were totally dependent on him."[1] C. E. Arnold helps illustrate this from the New Testament: "when Jesus made His triumphal entry into Jerusalem shortly before His passion, the crowds heralded His arrival by waving palm branches (John 12:13). The palm branches in the hands of the martyrs make a powerful statement of their triumph over the forces of evil. This multiethnic multitude now celebrates God and the Lamb for one primary benefit they have received—salvation."[2]

They're all shouting together! *Every ethnicity becomes charismatic in heaven!* Can you imagine getting your new body and being before God? I mean, He's right there! Jesus is sitting on His throne at the right hand of God the Father and He's right before you. You won't be thinking about, "I want to see what my momma's doing." You won't be asking about the giants in Genesis 6 or how the miracles happened. When you see Jesus and you see God the Father, you're going to shout!

The people are lifting up their voices with a voice of triumph. They are yelling! Why would God want this? God is not hard of hearing. And they're right before Him. So why would they shout right in front of God? God is not saying, "Shhh . . . ya'll are hurting my ears." They give Him all praise loudly because they're blown away by being in His presence. And He is worthy! God wants to be glorified to the corridors of every sector of this planet. He wants to be seen. He wants to be known. He's too big for just one language and just one people to worship Him.

What's so powerful about this is that Scripture says, "They cried out in a loud voice," even though there were multiple ethnicities there. "A" voice. Whether the people are all speaking in their own languages like people did on the Day of Pentecost or they are all speaking—with one heart and one mind—in singular, heavenly voice, everyone is lifting up, honoring, praising, and glorifying God's name. John saw the vast expanse of the people groups, heard their languages in worship, and knew that they were all saying, "Salvation belongs to our God, who is seated on the throne, and to the Lamb!" (Rev. 7:10).

Angels, Elders, and Four Living Creatures

Look at what happens next. All of the angels are standing around the throne and around the elders and around the four living creatures. So the angels, the elders, and the four living creatures are standing with the people of God who are saying, over and over again, "Salvation belongs to our God, who is seated on the throne, and to the Lamb." The angels and the elders and the four living creatures are amazed by what they're seeing.

The angels are in heaven after it's all over. They're looking at people they served. They're standing there remembering how much of a mess we were, how far away from God we were. How hooked on drugs we were. How sexually promiscuous we were. How proud we were. How idolatrous we were. How racist we were. And they look at God and they look at the people and they say, "Amen! Blessing and glory and wisdom. . . ." As a matter of fact, they fall on their faces. They're worshipping God because of His salvific work in saving you and me. They say, "Amen!" first—usually you say amen last—*Let everything we say be true.* Then they say, "Blessing" (*eulogia*), a praise of celebration to someone or some place. "Glory," which is an acknowledgement of all of God's glorious attributes. Then they say, "Wisdom," pointing to the fact that God saved us. The angels were there when Jesus left heaven, when heaven shook when He died on the cross, and when He left the tomb. And now they're there saying, "So this is what that was all about! I cannot believe that we get to experience the glory of what God was doing in those who were made lesser than us for a little while."

Those who were lesser become greater because of Jesus. But what does this have to do with race? What does this have to do with justice? What does this have to do with the gospel? Everything! If you know that all ethnicities are going to praise God together, how can you hate anyone?

Tribulation Saints

One of the elders explains to John the story of those who wore the white robes. These are the folks who survived the great tribulation. These are the ones who have gone through one of the most difficult times on the planet—they are different ethnicities, but they are unified. These folks who are there went through some things together. We should be like that. We should be able to work through this issue of injustice together. Hell shouldn't have to break loose before we break down some walls.

There will come a day when it won't be based on ethnicity. It's going to be based on you knowing Jesus. He said, "These are the ones coming out of the great tribulation. They washed their robes and made them white in the blood of the Lamb" (Rev. 7:14). That means everybody has to be equally cleaned by the blood of Jesus. I love this passage! He says, "For this reason they are before the throne of God, and they serve Him day and night in His temple. The one seated on the throne will shelter them" (Rev. 7:15). I can't wait!

Revelation 7:16–17a says, "They will no longer hunger; they will no longer thirst; the sun will no longer strike them, nor will any scorching heat. For the Lamb who is at the center of the throne will shepherd them." This is the fulfillment of Psalm 23 in its fullness: "The LORD is my Shepherd; I have what I need. He lets me lie down in green pastures; He leads me beside quiet waters." Likewise in Revelation 7:17b: "He will guide them to springs of the waters of life."

In eternity all of our needs will be satisfied. That means you won't have to worry about wanting to be married, not being able to pay the bills, a diagnosis of a terminal illness, being mistreated and disrespected. In other words, God is the everlasting fountain to satisfy. This doesn't start in eternity. When you draw close to Him, He will pour into you waters of life! In effect, Jesus told the woman at the well, "If you knew the gift of God and who was hollering at you right now, I'd have given you water that's greater than this. I'd have given you water so that you'd never thirst again!" The woman drops her bucket and says, "Lord, show me this water." And Jesus says, "I am He" (see John 4:13–26).

If we're going to engage the brokenness in our culture, we have to know how messed up we are, how great Jesus is, and how awesome the end is going to be. This is not cultural escapism to talk about the *eschaton*—it is the empowerment for the now. When you know you're messed up, you can look a racist in the face differently. It's got to be the living God that shows me myself, that shows me my brokenness, and lets me know that I've been forgiven. And because I've been forgiven much, how in the world can I withhold forgiveness from somebody else?

We may be surprised when we get to heaven to see that there are some saved militants, and there are saved racists. Racism doesn't make you lose your salvation. It's a sin among many other sins. And if racists know Jesus, they're going to be in heaven. They're going to be in that number that no man can number. Why not fight for reconciliation now? Why not fight to make sure that our interpersonal relationships as well as our churches mirror the reality that we'll experience in eternity?

Multiethnic Churches

If the church of today began to look like the future that Revelation speaks of, it would be the kind of witness that would literally rock the world. All churches don't have to be multiethnic, and we need to be fine with that. But if our churches are homogeneous, we must work to have a strong racial IQ. We must not let our ethnically homogeneous environments create a "them and us" atmosphere. Brothers and sisters who are in places where diversity is slim shouldn't be made to feel guilt or shame. When I was doing doctoral work in Boston, there were Ethiopian churches, Cambodian churches, Brazilian churches, Chinese churches, Nigerian churches, etc. From a mission standpoint, for these groups to attempt to merge for the sake of multiethnicity would be counter-productive. I would say this is also important for predominantly white and black churches within the same city. But it is important for every church to be on the spectrum from multiethnic-friendly to multiethnic.

Many believers are passionate about planting or transitioning their church to being multiethnic. I believe it is a great aspiration. Those who are in diverse contexts can foster this cross-ethnic revolution of the Woke Church. We will see the greatest revolution and revival in these contexts, with ethnic minorities leading in key positions and white brethren being willing to submit to qualified minorities. These minorities must have cross-cultural credibility. The witness of such a ministry will be mind-boggling to the world.

I can't tell you how powerful it has been at Epiphany Fellowship for people to see our diversity. We have planted fifteen churches overseas and eight churches in the United States. Almost all of our churches in the U.S. are multiethnic. Recently, I visited our Los Angeles church plant located in the Crenshaw section of the city in this old YMCA facility. On the hill behind the church are "The Hills," where some of the wealthiest blacks reside. Between the church and the Hills is "the jungles," a multiethnic neighborhood with economic challenges. Across the street from the church is a vast array of shopping options. When I entered the building, I saw Asians, Native Americans, whites, and blacks, of different ages and economic spheres, all setting up for worship. My breath was taken away as I mounted the sacred desk to preach in the most multiethnic church plant I'd seen to date.

We must understand, however, that this is only one aspect of the church—it's not *the* church. We have to encourage these types of ministries, without making it more central than Jesus and the gospel. As we seek to be with each other we must worship Jesus, not diversity. Keeping Jesus central is very important to the long-term depth of the Woke Church. Let's not allow the culture to beat us to realizing the vision the Bible already mapped out for the church. Diversity flows from the Bible, not from cultural tolerance. Manuel Ortiz explains the essential connection between doctrine and diversity.

> A multiethnic church in Denver discovered over a ten-year period that several elements were essential for an effective ministry bound by the gospel of reconciliation in a multi-ethnic community. There was a need to be intentional from the start. It was also necessary to have theological commitments that voiced the concern not only for multiethnicity but also for justice. These emphases had to be part of the doctrinal commitment of the church and incorporated into the training of new members.[3]

Every church needs to be engaged in key issues of justice, but multiethnic churches have the opportunity to lead the way. It isn't enough to be in the same room; we have to engage in the same mission. As difficult as this seems, engaging racial injustice can be a mechanism for reaching the lost and reinvigorating those who have left the church.

> It is clear to all of us who believe in the power of the gospel and the redeeming work of Christ that salvation is of the Lord. He alone gives the increase. But God uses the conditions of the world to bring people to Him through the preaching of the gospel. Demographics tell us what to expect as we think about the future of the church. The world continues to change rapidly, and we need to know how to use cultural changes and flows of people for the furtherance of the gospel. It is the Christian's responsibility to be faithful to the world in which we live and to the Word of God that gives life. In a world where many people are heading toward the cities, who will welcome them? And in the United States, how shall we prepare for the continued migration pull into this country?[4]

My prayer and hope is that the multiethnic church will not be a fad, but one of the many church community formation options that break barriers and chains to the glory of Jesus. The multiethnic church encourages me. It is a foretaste of what heaven will look like. And I can't wait for that moment.

WHEN JESUS RETURNS

Few scenes in the Bible can compete with Revelation 19–20. Jesus will end His fast from the fruit of the vine. At the marriage feast, the church will no longer be betrothed to Jesus (2 Cor. 11:2–3).

We, as the bride of Christ, will be married to our Savior. He will mount His white horse and enter earth's atmosphere with a name tattooed on His thigh and embroidered on His robe with highlights of red blood in the robe accompanied by the host of heaven. We will be raised with Him to judge and reign with Him. Our unified multiethnic community will be together in our ethnic differences but in one accord.

He will land on the Mount of Olives, and it will split from east to west and the second epiphany and advent of our Lord will begin. I love the way John describes our soon-coming King in Revelation 19:11–16:

> Then I saw heaven opened, and there was a white
> horse. Its rider is called Faithful and True, and he
> judges and makes war with justice. His eyes were like
> a fiery flame, and many crowns were on his head. He
> had a name written that no one knows except himself.
> He wore a robe dipped in blood, and his name is called
> the Word of God. The armies that were in heaven
> followed him on white horses, wearing pure white
> linen. A sharp sword came from his mouth, so that he
> might strike the nations with it. He will rule them with
> an iron rod. He will also trample the winepress of the
> fierce anger of God, the Almighty. And he has a name
> written on his robe and on his thigh: KING OF KINGS
> AND LORD OF LORDS.

This will mark the true end of days and the beginning of new ones. We will be forever on the New Earth, and Jesus will accomplish in one moment all that we have been striving toward. All corrupt authorities and systems will be called into full account. The King of Justice will exact His vengeance on those inflicted by these evils and more. Those who know the Son of God will be rewarded and receive eternal restitution for their suffering. On this day there will be no more injustice, police brutality, racism, classism, poverty, cancer, marches, riots, wars, hatred, killing, segregation, slavery, crying, dying, sickness, hospitals, inequities, or brokenness, but Jesus will be all in all. As Paul states, Jesus will hand the kingdom back over to the Father:

> Then comes the end, when he hands over the kingdom to God the Father, when he abolishes all rule and all authority and power. For he must reign until he puts all his enemies under his feet. The last enemy to be abolished is death. For God has put everything under his feet. Now when it says "everything" is put under him, it is obvious that he who puts everything under him is the exception. When everything is subject to Christ, then the Son himself will also be subject to the one who subjected everything to him, so that God may be all in all. (1 Cor. 15:24–28)

God the Father's tabernacle will reside on earth, and Jesus will take His rightful seat beside Him in full sight of all! And we will worship Yahweh and Yeshua as the one God in the Holy Spirit forever and ever!

If the church can keep this image of what is to come before us, we will be energized to work to accomplish His purposes in the earth. We will work as one unified body, across all ethnic lines. When the Philadelphia Eagles won the Super Bowl, people in the city of Philadelphia flooded the streets. There was a celebration like never before. They were all wearing one jersey: the Eagles team jersey. Philly is a very racially divided city, from Little Italy, to the Black Sunni Salafee orthodox Muslims of 52nd

Street, to the Chinese in China Town. However, on that day, everyone—almost one million people—forgot their differences and flooded the streets of Philadelphia. They forgot about all of their differences and all of their frustrations, because the ones who had won the game represented all of the people of Philly. Instead of fighting each other, they gathered around the ones who won the game for them, forgetting that they ever had differences.

When Jesus returns, the global multiethnic church will have on the same white jersey. We will put away our differences and with one voice will shout together,

> Salvation belongs to our God,
> who is seated on the throne,
> and to the Lamb! (Rev. 7:10)

> Hallelujah!
> Salvation, glory, and power belong to our God,
> because his judgments are true and righteous,
> because he has judged the notorious prostitute
> who corrupted the earth with her sexual immorality;
> and he has avenged the blood of his servants
> that was on her hands.

A second time they said,

> Hallelujah!
> Her smoke ascends forever and ever! (Rev. 19:1–3)

This, my friends, is the Woke Church!

ACKNOWLEDGMENTS

I'd like to thank the good Lord for giving me the endurance to write this work. This has been my most sanctifying book to write.

Also thankful for my wife and her giving me the space to work on this and deal with my varied emotions through the process. So many days and nights you have seen me carrying a library worth of books. To my children, who I had in mind as I wrote this, because of the present they live in and the future that they are headed to.

Thanks to Epiphany Fellowship Church and the pastors for granting me the space to explore the issues of justice and racism and standing with me. Your support and encouragement has been amazing. Let's continue to fight to show off the glory of Christ in every area of life. Thanks to Dr. Tiffany Gill for reading over the historical portion of the book and giving me feedback. Thanks as well to Jeremiah Carr, my assistant, and to Ladesha Albury, who along with Thriving, has carried the Woke Church brand for two years.

Thankful to Moody Publishers for jumping at the chance to do this book. From Drew, Jeremy, Erik, Connor, the whole team. Can't forget Mrs. Karen Waddles. Your editing made it feel like we were working on an album. To the rest of the Moody staff and company. Blessings.

NOTES

CHAPTER 1: THE CHURCH SHOULD ALREADY BE WOKE

1. Mary Bagley, "Kilauea Volcano: Facts About the 30-Year Eruption," May 8, 2018, Live Science, https://www.livescience.com/27622-kilauea.html.

2. J. Swanson, *Dictionary of Biblical Languages with Semantic Domains: Greek (New Testament)*, electronic ed. (Oak Harbor: Logos Research Systems, Inc:, 1997), 476.

3. Nima Elbagin, Raja Raxek, Alex Platt, and Bryony Jones, CNN Special Report: "People for Sale: Where Lives are Auctioned for $400," https://www.cnn.com/2017/11/14/africa/libya-migrant-auctions/index.html.

4. "Are You Woke? Angela Rye, Luvvie Ajaye, April Reign and April Ryan Talk about the Real Meaning of the Word," Essence, July 1, 2017, http://www.essence.com/festival/2017-essence-festival/angela-rye-luvvie-ajaye-april-reign-april-ryan-woke.

5. W. E. B. Du Bois, *The Souls of Black Folk*, (2012-05-16), Kindle Edition, 5.

6. Brian Loritts, *Right Color, Wrong Culture* (Chicago: Moody Publishers, 2014), 198.

7. "What is an Evangelical?," National Association of Evangelicals website, https://www.nae.net/what-is-an-evangelical/.

8. J. P. Louw and E. A. Nida, *Greek-English Lexicon of the New Testament: Based on Semantic Domains*, electronic ed. of the 2nd edition, vol. 1 (New York: United Bible Societies, 1996), 662.

CHAPTER 2: HOW BIG IS THE GOSPEL? (JUSTICE AND THE GOSPEL)

1. Tony Evans, *Oneness Embraced: Reconciliation, the Kingdom, and How We are Stronger Togethe*r (Chicago: Moody Publishers, 2011), 266.

2. Anthony A. Hoekema, *Saved by Grace* (Grand Rapids, MI: Wm. B. Eerdmans, 1994), loc. 2236-39, Kindle.

3. Fleming Rutledge, *The Crucifixion: Understanding the Death of Jesus Christ* (Grand Rapids, MI: Wm. B. Eerdmans, 2015), 327–28 (Kindle Edition).

4. Ibid., 328–29 (Kindle Edition).

5. R. T. France, *The Gospel of Matthew* (Grand Rapids, MI: Wm. B. Eerdmans, 2007), 873.

6. Peter Holmes and Sidney Thelwall, *The Sacred Writings of Tertullian, Vol. 1* (Germany: Jazzybee Verlag, 2017), 360.

7. Lois Barrett, *Missional Church: A Vision for the Sending of the Church in North America*, The Gospel and Our Culture Series (Grand Rapids, MI: Wm. B. Eerdmans, 1998), loc. 92–93, Kindle.

8. Tim Keller, "How Biblical Shalom Resembles a Beautiful Fabric," Preaching Today, http://www.preachingtoday.com/illustrations/2010/november/7111510.html.

9. Nicholas Wolterstorff, *Until Justice and Peace Embrace* (Grand Rapids, MI: Wm. B. Eerdman's Publishing, 1983), 69–71.

10. Darrell Guder, *The Incarnation and the Church's Witness* (Eugene, OR: Wipf & Stock Publications, 2005), xii.

11. "A Love without Condition," *History of the Early Church* (blog), earlychurch.com/unconditional-love.php.

CHAPTER 3: WE'RE FAMILY, WE'RE HOLY

1. John M. Perkins, *One Blood: Parting Words to the Church on Race* (Chicago: Moody Publishers, 2018), 166–67.

CHAPTER 4: IS THE CHURCH ASLEEP?

1. "The Transatlantic Slave Trade," Understanding Slavery Initiative, http://www.understandingslavery.com/index.php-option=com_content&view=article&id=369&Itemid=145.html.

2. Mark Galli, "Slaveholding Evangelist: Whitefield's Troubling Mix of Views," *Christianity Today*, 1993.

3. Thabiti Anyabwile, "Jonathan Edwards, Slavery, and the Theology of African Americans," paper presented February 1, 2012 at Trinity Evangelical Divinity School.

4. Craig S. Keener and Glenn Usry, *Defending Black Faith: Answers to Tough Questions about African-American Christianity* (Downers Grove, IL: InterVarsity Press Academic, 1997), 33.

5. Albert J. Raboteau, *Slave Religion: The Invisible Institution in the Antebellum South* (Oxford, England: Oxford University Press, 2004), 103.

6. "Nat Turner," History.com, http://www.history.com/topics/black-history/nat-turner.

7. Eugene G. Genovese, *Roll, Jordan, Roll: The World the Slave Made* (New York: Vintage Press, 1976), 186.

8. Cornel West and Eddie Glaude, Jr., gen. ed., "Black Conversion and White Sensibility," *African American Religious Thought: An Anthology* (Louisville, KY: Westminster John Knox Press, 2003), 294–95.

9. George M. Fredrickson, *Racism: A Short History (Princeton Classics)* (Princeton, NJ: Princeton University Press, 2015), Kindle Locations 462–469.

10. Eric S. Jacobson, "Silent observer or silent partner: Methodism and the Texas Ku Klux Klan, 1921–1925." *Methodist History* 31, no. 2 (1993): 104. Source of quote within quote: Robert Moats Miller, "A Note on the Relationship Between the Protestant Churches and the Revived Ku Klux Klan," Journal of Southern History 22 (August 1956).

11. Kelly J. Baker, "Religion and the Rise of the Second Ku Klux Klan, 1915–1922," http://www.readex.com/readex-report/religion-and-rise-second-ku-klux-klan-1915-1922.

12. "Black Wall Street," Greenwood Cultural Center, http://www.greenwoodculturalcenter.com/black-wall-street.

13. Samer Rao, "It's Been 96 Years Since White Mobs Destroyed Tulsa's Black Wall Street," Colorlines online magazine, May 31, 2017, https://www.colorlines.com/articles/its-been-96-years-white-mobs-destroyed-tulsas-black-wall-street.

14. Hannibal B. Johnson, *Black Wall Street: From Riot to Renaissance in Tulsa's Historic Greenwood District* (Woodway, TX: Eakin Press, 2014), loc. 1400–1401, Kindle.

15. Alan Bean, "The African-American Roots of Bonhoeffer's Christianity," Baptist News Global, October 30, 2015, https://baptistnews.com/article/the-african-american-roots-of-bonhoeffers-christianity/#.Wz5XY9VKiUl.

16. Dietrich Bonhoeffer, "Protestantism without the Reformation," in *No Rusty Swords: Letters, Lectures and Notes, 1928–1936*, ed. Edwin H. Robertson, trans. Edwin H. Robertson and John Bowden (London: Collins, 1965), 92–118. As cited by Michael Horton in *Who Exactly Are the Evangelicals?*

17. Martin Luther King Jr., "Letter from a Birmingham Jail," African Studies Center, University of Pennsylvania, http://www.africa.upenn.edu/Articles_Gen/Letter_Birmingham.html.

18. "Emmitt Till: Biography," Biography.com, https://www.biography.com/people/emmett-till-507515.

19. Barry Hankins, "The Family Feud that Changed the Shape of Christian Higher Education," *Christianity Today,* May 17, 2018, https://www.christianitytoday.com/ct/2018/may-web-only/adam-laats-fundamentalist-u.html?utm_source=leadership-html.

20. Lecrae, "Facts about Lecrae," Truth's Table podcast, September 30, 2017, https://overcast.fm/+IkU79eRbY/.

21. Tony Evans, *Oneness Embraced: Reconciliation, the Kingdom, and How We Are Stronger Together* (Chicago: Moody Publishers, 2011), 183–84.

22. Chris Brooks, "American Slavery-Segregation Chart," used by permission.

CHAPTER 5: THINGS FOR THE CHURCH TO LAMENT

1. William Andrews, *Book of Lamentations,* in *The Lexham Bible Dictionary,* J. D. Barry, D. Bomar, D. R. Brown, R. Klippenstein, D. Mangum, C. Sinclair Wolcott, W. Widder, eds. (Bellingham, WA: Lexham Press, 2016).

2. Richard Allen, *The Life, Experience, and Gospel Labours of the Rt. Rev. Richard Allen* (Seattle: Amazon Digital Services, 2010), loc. 132–42, Kindle.

3. Barbara Skinner, "Been There, Done That," *Reconciler* magazine, Winter 1996, 4.

4. Bryan Loritts, "More on Leaving White Evangelicalism: A Response by Bryan Loritts," *Christianity Today* web site, posted October 17, 2017, http://www.christianitytoday.com/edstetzer/2017/october/response-to-ray-changs-open-letter-to-john-piper.html.

5. Thomas C. Oden. *How Africa Shaped the Christian Mind: Rediscovering the African Seedbed of Western Christianity* (Downers Grove, IL: InterVarsity Press, 2015), loc. 460–64, Kindle.

6. Jared Alcantara, "Mourning the Loss of the Last Pulpit Prince," *Christianity Today,* April, 2015, https://www.christianitytoday.com/pastors/2015/april-online-only/mourning-loss-of-last-pulpit-prince.html.

7. "Herstory," Black Lives Matter, https://blacklivesmatter.com/about/herstory/.

8. Ibid.

CHAPTER 6: RECLAIMING OUR PROPHETIC VOICE

1. R. B. Y. Scott, "Is Preaching Prophecy?," *Canadian Journal of Theology,* I (Toronto: University of Toronto Press, April, 1955), 11–18.

2. David R. Helm, *Expositional Preaching: How We Speak God's Word Today* (9Marks: Building Healthy Churches) (Wheaton, IL: Crossway, 2014), loc. 138–39, Kindle.

3. Crystal Blanton, "Inspiration, Reflection and Justice: Spirituality through the Voices of Our Leaders," Feb. 5, 2013, *Daughters of Eve* (blog), Patheos, http://www.patheos.com/blogs/daughtersofeve/2013/02/inspiration-reflection-and-justice-spirituality-through-the-voices-of-our-leaders/.

4. Ibid.

5. C. Eric Lincoln and Lawrence H. Mamiya, *The Black Church in the African American Experience* (Durham, NC: Duke University Press, 1990), loc. 4329-37, Kindle.

CHAPTER 7: A VISION FOR CHANGE

1. Mark Fazlollah, Craig R. McCoy & Jeremy Roebuck, "Philadelphia DA's Office Keeps Secret List of Police," The Inquirer: Philly.com, February 13, 2018, http://www.philly.com/philly/news/philadelphia-police-misconduct-list-larry-krasner-seth-williams-meek-mill-20180213.html.

2. Tanea Jackson, "Nelson Mandela Accepts Honorary Doctorate Degree from Six Institutions in the Laureate International Universities Network," Laureate International Universities, June 5, 2010, https://www.laureate.net/newsroom/pressreleases/2010/05/nelsonmandelaaccepts honorarydoctorate.

3. Marilyn Elias, "The School to Prison Pipeline," Tolerance Online Magazine, Spring 2013 issue, http://www.tolerance.org/sites/default/files/general/School-to-Prison.pdf.

4. Seth Gershenson, Cassandra Hart, Constance Lindsey, "With Just One Black Teacher, Black Students More Likely to Graduate," John Hopkins University, April 5, 2017, http://releases.jhu.edu/2017/04/05/with-just-one-black-teacher-black-students-more-likely-to-graduate/.

5. Emma Brown, "White Teachers and Black Teachers Have Different Expectations for Black Students," *The Washington Post*, March 31, 2016, https://www.washingtonpost.com/news/education/wp/2016/03/31/white-teachers-and-black-teachers-have-different-expectations-for-black-students/?noredirect=on&utm_term=.58483adde910.

CHAPTER 8: THE WOKE CHURCH IN ACTION

1. Tony Evans, *Oneness Embraced: Reconciliation, the Kingdom, and How We Are Stronger Together* (Chicago: Moody Publishers, 2011), 184.

2. Soong-Chan Rah, *Many Colors: Cultural Intelligence for a Changing Church* (Chicago: Moody Publishers, 2010), loc. 2329–39, Kindle.

3. "History," Gacaca Community Justice, http://gacaca.rw/about/history-3/.

4. Ibid.

5. "German Soldiers React to Footage of Concentration Camps, 1945," Rare Historical Photos.com, https://rarehistoricalphotos.com/german-soldiers-forced-watch-footage-concentration-camps-1945/.

6. "Sankofa," The Evangelical Covenant Church, http://www.covchurch.org/justice/racial-righteousness/sankofa/.

7. Psalm 127:1, note 3, *The NET Bible,* first edition (Biblical Studies Press, 2005).

8. Willie Richardson, *Reclaiming the Urban Family* (Grand Rapids, MI: Zondervan Publishing, 1996), 27–29.

9. Tony Evans, *The Kingdom Agenda* (Chicago: Moody Publishers, 2006), 217.

10. Tiffany Johnson, "Female Dignity" (article written as contribution to *Woke Church*).

11. Sarita T. Lyons, "Female Dignity" (article written as contribution to *Woke Church*).

12. Eric Mason, *Manhood Restored: How the Gospel Makes Men Whole* (Nashville: Broadman & Holman Publishing Company, 2013), 138.

13. "33, The Series," Authentic Manhood, https://www.authenticman hood.com/.

14. Michelle Alexander, *The New Jim Crow* (New York: The New Press, 2012), 98–99.

CHAPTER 9: SEEING THROUGH THE LENS OF THE END

1. Craig S. Keener, *The IVP Bible Background Commentary: New Testament,* second edition (Downers Grove, IL: InterVarsity Press, 2014), 744.

2. Clinton E. Arnold, *Zondervan Illustrated Bible Backgrounds Commentary: Hebrews to Revelation* (Grand Rapids, MI: Zondervan, 2002), 296.

3. Harvie M. Conn and Manuel Ortiz, *Urban Ministry: The Kingdom, the City & the People of God* (Downers Grove, IL: InterVarsity Press, 2010), loc. 3515–18, Kindle.

4. Ibid.

WORDS OF WISDOM TO THE NEXT GENERATION FROM A PIONEER OF THE CIVIL RIGHTS MOVEMENT

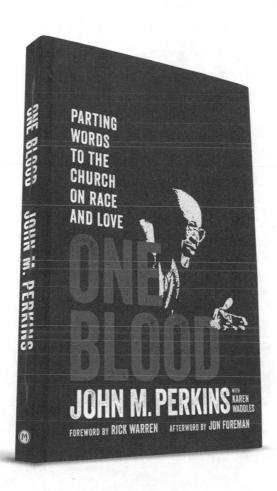

In this his crowning work, Dr. Perkins speaks honestly to the church about—in his own words—"the things I've discovered to be crucial about reconciliation, discipleship, and justice... the principles I believe to be vital to a complete ministry of reconciliation." Here is a final manifesto from a man whose life's work has been reconciliation.

978-0-8024-1801-2 | also available as an eBook

RECONCILIATION, THE KINGDOM, AND HOW WE ARE STRONGER TOGETHER

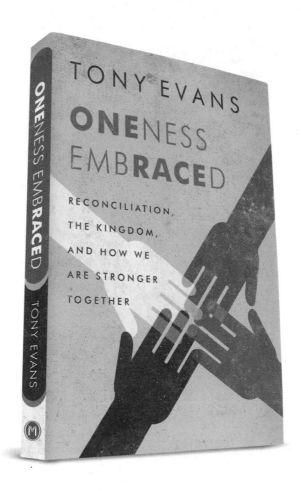